Your First Year in Ministry

What They Didn't Teach
You in Seminary

GLYN NORMAN

CONTENTS

DEDICATION

This book is dedicated to my beautiful wife Cathleen and my wonderful children, Landon and Cicely.

GLYN NORMAN

ACKNOWLEDGMENTS

Thanks also to the following:

John Glass, who lived the gospel, and first invited me to church;

John Bishop, my first pastor at Tankerton Evangelical Church (TEC), who believed in me and got my hands dirty in ministry;

TEC friends, who encouraged this baby Christian in his first steps and picked me up when I fell;

Chip Kirk, my mentor and friend, who has shared his very life with me, and I am richer for it;

My professors at London Bible College (now London School of Theology), particularly Conrad Gempf, Deryck Sheriffs and Peter Cotterell, who transmitted a love of learning and theology to me that continues to this day;

My congregations at University Praise/Sojourners Community Church in California and South Tampa Fellowship in Florida, whom I have had the immense privilege of pastoring;

And my Lord and Savior Jesus Christ, whose love for me and patience with me continue to astonish me.

Glyn Norman,
Tampa, FL   June 28, 2012

INTRODUCTION

A friend of mine, who is ex-military, recently introduced me to a new term that he learned during his time in the Air Force. The term is: "The Gouge." "The Gouge" refers to the body of knowledge that was not part of the official briefing but which would be essential for the success of the mission. That is why I wrote this book.

In almost every vocation, there is a gap between what you learn at college and what you actually need to know to get the job done well. In the context of ministry, many theological colleges and seminaries do a wonderful job of teaching the budding pastor biblical and historical theology, church history, Greek, exegesis, and sermon preparation. In real ministry though, you will face problems and situations for which you were never trained. Naturally, I hope you have a baseline belief that God will provide what you lack in such situations, but some additional wisdom from someone who has served on the front lines may also be helpful and welcome.

5

- ◆ What do you do when someone you are counseling is draining you emotionally and keeps coming back for more?
- ◆ How do you prepare a sermon when you have an "open door" policy and keep getting interrupted with "trivial" matters?
- ◆ How do you balance the various demands on your time?
- ◆ How do you prioritize what is most important?
- ◆ How can you make a funeral or a wedding meaningful and personal for those involved?

This small book seeks to be "The Gouge" for those and other situations.

First, though, a couple of disclaimers: Since the vast majority of pastors are male, I have used male pronouns throughout this book. That should not be interpreted as anything other than an attempt to avoid awkwardness of grammar and sentence construction that would have occurred with an attempt to be gender inclusive. If you are a woman reading this book, I think you will find much that is helpful, and I apologize for your "on-the-fly" conversion of "he" and "his" to "her" and hers" that will be necessary.

Second, this book is not intended to cover every possible situation. Such a volume would be a vast and intimidating tome, and certainly beyond my ability to write. My hope is that it helps you avoid some pitfalls of ministry by reading about them, rather than learning through painful mistakes. If you become aware of a major gap in this book, please let me know, and I'll consider covering it in a later edition.

Lastly, please don't see this book as a criticism,

implicit or explicit, of theological colleges or seminaries. I am a product of one myself, and I hold my time there, and what I learned, in the highest esteem. This is designed to be an supplement to what you learned there, and in no way any kind of replacement.

My hope and prayer is that you will find a few things that will make the transition from seminary to church a little smoother and your early days of ministry more effective.

GLYN NORMAN

CHAPTER 1:
LANDING YOUR FIRST JOB

The natural first priority as you are nearing the end of your Bible college or seminary time is to gain a position in ministry. This section should help you decide what avenue to pursue and develop an effective strategy to get the position you want.

What Are You Looking for?

I do not take it for granted that every person graduating from Bible college or seminary wishes to become a pastor. Some simply wish to gain a deeper theological education. Others perhaps want to pursue missions or some other calling. For the purposes of this guide however, I will assume that the majority do wish to become pastors, and it is primarily for them that this guide is written.

Simply put, you have to know what you are looking for, and you have to be sure that the way you are wired (spiritual gifting, experience, personality, natural abilities, passion) suits the position you are seeking. That requires an honest self-evaluation, and it may also be helpful to seek the advice of others. Ask them, "In what area of ministry can you envision me being most successful?" and listen carefully to how they answer. You may imagine yourself as a hotshot, inspirational preacher, but your friends who have heard your teaching, and know your skills, might indicate that you would be wiser seeking an "executive pastor"-type position rather than a position that involves a great deal of teaching.

It is critically important for you to be honest with yourself, and to ask others to be honest with you. Far better to receive "wounds from a friend" than have a search committee tell you that you are completely unsuitable for the position you want. Once you have decided on a specific position to pursue, you can move to the next phase.

You will also need to decide on your geographical and cultural preferences. A Southern Baptist church in Alabama is likely to have a very different feel than a non-denominational church in San Francisco. Where do you fit culturally? Are you best suited to a more conservative environment, or a more innovative, less traditional environment? Do you prefer to minister in an environment where most people have heard the gospel, or where most haven't? Can you communicate effectively to those "on the outside," or are you more adept with those already within the church environment? In certain parts of the country, certain churches may have strong political leanings toward one party. Are you comfortable with that? A socially liberal-leaning, Democratic-voting pastor might fit wonderfully in some parts of California but would struggle in some conservative churches in the South that are predominantly Republican and socially very conservative in their outlook.

The answers to those questions may dictate geographical and church preferences.

The Search

There are two main avenues for becoming aware of ministry positions. One is through personal networking, and the other is through the Internet, usually by means of a dedicated pastoral search site. In terms of personal networking, it may be helpful to let your friends and acquaintances know that you will be seeking a position in the near future, and ask them to inform you if they know of anything that might be suitable. If they are in a position to recommend you for an open position, that gives you a head start above all the other resumés that the search committee will receive, since it comes with a personal endorsement from someone they know and probably trust.

As far as the Internet goes, there are a number of sites to check:

- ◆ ChurchStaffing.com (the primary search site for pastor jobs in the United States)
- ◆ ChurchJobs.net

Those two sites probably cover 90 percent of pastoral positions available in the United States, and sometimes beyond.

Also, if you are interested in a particular denomination, check out that denomination's specific website, because positions may be advertised there that are not posted elsewhere.

If you find a position that interests you, do some research. Often a more detailed description of the position is available on the church's own website, as well as other useful information such as demographics, the history of the church, governance and other useful information. Even the style of a church's website can tell you something.

Of particular interest, if it's available, is the doctrinal statement of the church. Read it carefully. If you find that the church has a doctrinal position with which you do not agree (women's roles in ministry, the use of spiritual gifts, etc.), then do not apply. It may be tempting to "fake it," and reason to yourself that you can disagree on some issues and it probably won't matter – but it will. Your true position will be found out, or you will be forced to uphold a position you don't truly support, and thus have to live with your own hypocrisy. It's just not worth it.

Your Internet Footprint

If you are conducting research on a church via the Internet and the church starts to consider you as a serious candidate, then the church is likely to do the same with you. Prior to this happening is a good time to do an internet audit of yourself. Type your name into Google and see what comes up. Check all the links that refer to you. Is there anything on Facebook, a blog, LinkedIn, etc., that might compromise your application? If so, take steps to correct it or remove it. Sometimes a provocative post, or picture, taken out of context can effectively cut you out of the running. You may know you were only drinking root beer at that party, but your prospective employer doesn't!

The Resumé

Most of what I share here may be obvious, but I

don't want to omit something simply because it seems obvious to me.

1. **Whatever you write must be true.** Every resumé shapes the truth to present a situation or achievement in its best light, but more than that is unethical and misleading. Your resumé must be the truth about you. Most churches will check the details and call previous employers or coworkers to verify the information you've given on the resumé. If what you said fails to verify, your application is over. Clearly, honesty is a virtue that one should be able to take for granted with a pastor.

2. **Your resumé should be free of written and grammatical errors.** The church is assuming that since you are intending to make a great first impression, your resumé is representative of your best work. A resumé that is sloppy or full of errors indicates a lack of attention to detail and will not impress a search committee.

3. **The resumé should be no longer than two pages.** If you have limited work experience prior to seminary/Bible college, then one page may be enough. However, if you are coming to ministry a little later in life, then more room may be needed to adequately represent your breadth of experience.

4. **When you are describing previous work/ ministry experience, try to do so in terms of accomplishments, not areas of responsibility**. To give a more secular

example, stating that you "Cut costs by 30% in first year of operation" is much stronger than "Responsible for departmental budget." Churches are interested in what you have done more than what you were responsible for.

5. **Tailor the resumé to the job.** Don't just use a generic resumé for every application. Some job descriptions, for example, may stress that the church is looking for someone who can work well as part of a team. If you know that is a high priority for the church, let it be reflected as a high priority for you in your resumé. If "Developed an effective multi-national team" was fourth on your list, perhaps you want to move it to first or second, so that the church can see quickly that the skills and experience you offer match its priorities. Burying something that is important deep down in the resumé is not wise, especially since the search team may only spend 30 seconds scanning each one.

6. In these Internet-savvy, multimedia days, it may be worthwhile to **add links to online media that show your preaching/teaching/worship leading.** I have an online version of my resumé that includes such links. Alternatively, you could include a CD/DVD with your resumé. Watching a video of you online for 5 minutes can tell a search committee a great deal about you – again, audit your online presence so that those links help your cause, rather than hinder it. Almost every church requires at least an

audio example of your preaching, so make sure those are easy to access. A dead or inaccurate link does not impress, and you don't want to start your application by frustrating the search committee, who may be dealing with dozens of other candidates.

The Cover Letter

Almost all churches request a cover letter to be sent with a resumé. Again, do not send a standard cover letter. Make sure you tailor it to the specific church and to the specific position you are seeking.

Early on in the cover letter, identify something about the church or position that resonated with you. If the church's description meets a passion or strongly held belief of yours, mention that. If the church's values are the same as yours, identify that and comment on it. Phrases such as, "What drew me to apply for this position was your strongly held commitment to reaching the lost. This is a value that is extremely important to me, demonstrated by ..."

In that way, you are showing that your are not sending just a generic cover letter, but an introduction from someone who values what the church values.

References

Churches are becoming ever more diligent in checking references. It is not unknown for some churches to hire staffing consultants who check references for them, sometimes with extensive telephone interviews of up to an hour with each reference.

Try to choose references who are not purely personal but who have worked with you in some capacity. The church interested in you wants to know not only that you have a wonderful personality, but also what you are like to work with. If possible, choose as references people who supervised you, who were co-workers, and perhaps some who you supervised.

Although it may seem like "stacking the deck," it may be worthwhile, when asking people if they are willing to be references, to mention to them the qualities the church seems to value highly. In that way they may be able to guide the conversation toward mentioning your applicable strengths for this position. An e-mail to your references, before they are contacted, will help your references know what situations to mention, and which of your many virtues to extol. In the e-mail you might say something such as, "This church is interested in my ability as a creative Bible teacher and as a team player."

The Interviews

At a certain point in the process, there will be an interview. More and more churches are using phone interviews and/or video interviews via Skype prior to meeting a candidate in person. Following are some tips that will help you prepare for the interviews.

For a phone interview, don't let the fact that they can't see you put you in a casual state of mind (or dress). Even though I could do a phone interview in my pajamas, I try to dress in the clothing that I would wear for an "in-person" interview, so that my frame of mind and mentality are sufficiently formal for the nature of the conversation. I prefer to sit at a desk, and since it is a phone interview, I can make use of "cheat sheets" with key things I need to know about the church or want to include in the conversation to demonstrate my strengths in certain areas.

Naturally, the same would apply to a Skype interview in terms of dress, but your notes will have to be more carefully placed within your sight line behind the video camera. For both scenarios, make sure you are in a quiet location that will be free from interruption, and arrange a back-up plan by e-mail or instant messaging if the technology doesn't work. A simple paragraph such as this shows that you are a contingency planner:

"I look forward to speaking with you on Skype on (date/time). My Skype ID is _____. If for any reason we have problems with the connection, please call me on my home phone, (_____).

Much of what applies to the cover letter also applies to the interview. The church will have given you quite a few clues in the job description about what it is looking for. If you are given a natural opportunity to demonstrate how you fit that specification, then do so. For each of your points, It is useful to have a mini-narrative that demonstrates that this is not just a philosophical assent on your part, but something you actually practice.

For example, the church may have said in its job description that "the pastor should be someone who, through his example, mentors others." Rather than simply say, "I think mentoring is a great idea, and I'm all for it," be more specific with a truthful example from your current situation: "I was interested that you value mentoring so highly. That's something that's very important to me, too, and I currently meet weekly with three men in a discipleship group. We are studying _____ together, and it's thrilling to see each of us growing through this experience." Such an answer demonstrates more clearly that mentoring is a value for which you "walk the walk" and don't just "talk the talk."

Try to develop mini-narratives for each area of strength that may be discussed – creative teaching, pastoral care, working with difficult people, dealing with conflict, etc. We are hardwired to remember stories better than propositional statements, and you can be sure that you will stand out as a candidate if you back up your assertions with a brief demonstration of how you live it out. However, don't be long-winded. Three sentences should suffice to make the point. Don't drag it on unless a situation really requires a more detailed explanation, and even then, ask permission: "I'd like to explain how I've come to this position on that question, but it will take a couple of minutes. Would that be OK?"

Also prepare a mini-narrative for areas of weakness. Almost every interviewer will ask about areas in which you are weak. Don't be afraid of that question. The key, and hopefully the truth, is that the weakness you state is not critical or fatal for the position you're seeking.

What's important is to acknowledge the weakness but to frame it in such a way that turns it to the positive. Let's imagine that you suffer from impatience. You could simply say, "Sometimes I'm a little impatient" and leave it at that. If you do, it is up to the committee members to fill in the mental gaps regarding what that looks like, and their imagining could be worse that your reality. Far better to say, "I suffer a little from impatience when I feel meetings are dragging on and not accomplishing anything. I'm working on it by asking a colleague to keep me accountable for that, and by spending a few minutes before meetings praying particularly for patience." That's an equally honest answer but presents you as a person that is 1) self-aware and 2) willing to work on a weakness. Those two things in themselves are valuable in any candidate.

What you must not do is present something as an apparent weakness that is really a thinly disguised strength. Statements such as "I sometimes worry that I work too hard" or "Sometimes I think I care too much" are simply self-aggrandizing and insincere, and any decent interviewer will treat such statements with the disdain they deserve.

As far as the in-person interview goes, the typical wisdom applies. I tend to dress the same way I would if I were preaching at that church. If you can see from the website, or sermon videos, that the pastor wears a suit and tie to preach, that is how you should dress for the interview. If it's a more relaxed environment, then dress accordingly. If in doubt, go slightly more formal. It's OK to be slightly overdressed for an interview, but worse to be underdressed.

In your answers, maintain good eye contact, positive posture and an upbeat tone as much as possible. Remind yourself that these people want you to do well, to meet their expectations, to fit their specifications. They hope you will. They are for you and not against you, and they are providing an opportunity for you to show them who you are. Use humor if it is appropriate and part of your normal personality. If it isn't you, don't force it.

At the end of the interview, the person or panel usually will ask if you have any questions. It is good if you can prepare a question or two that demonstrate your interest and understanding of the situation you might be facing. It would be good to ask something like, "What would you consider to be the greatest challenges the church is facing at this time?" Generally, avoid questions about salary and/or benefits unless the interviewers introduce the subject first. That is best discussed when they have decided that you are the one they want and thus are perhaps more flexible regarding the package available.

CHAPTER 2:
DEALING WITH EXPECTATIONS

Expectations are a potential minefield for a new pastor. You immediately have to juggle your own expectations of yourself in this new role, plus the expectations of others, not forgetting to factor in the expectations of God Himself. As you will soon realize, there are two types of expectations: spoken and unspoken, or formal and implicit. It is necessary to manage both types well in order to remain effective and, more importantly, sane!

Your Own Expectations

Your expectations of yourself can vary widely according to your personality type. A Type A personality may have "conquer the world by next Wednesday" expectations, whereas a Type B may be more along the lines of "I hope I manage to do something useful here within the next five years." Whatever your style, it is important that your expectations of yourself are appropriate and realistic.

"Appropriate" means that there is a match between your personal capacity and the demands of the role. "Realistic" means that you have a sober estimation of your own abilities and what you can achieve. As Romans 12:3 says, you are "not to think of yourself more highly than you ought to think," and equally, do not underestimate yourself.

One thing I have learned is that most ministry is incremental. It moves along inches, rather than miles, at a time. Occasionally God will bless with a powerful advance, but ministry is oftentimes simply about faithful "plodding," continuing to fulfill the calling for which God chose you, one step at a time. It may not be very dramatic or impressive, but those things have inherent dangers anyway, of pride and overreaching. One preacher I know compares preaching to building a house. He says that usually it's one brick at a time, as though you are building a wall. Occasionally, you come to a window, and the God's sunlight beams through in a glorious display, but then the next week, you are back to brick by brick. The same can be said of much of ministry.

I must admit that, in my 20s, I would not have been satisfied to hear that ministry is mostly incremental. I sought the breakthrough, the dramatic advance, the massive Kingdom-building momentum. Sometimes that does happen – and sometimes the personnel involved are stars that flare brightly for a brief moment and then fade out, or fall away because of some failure in ministry or morality. If we are to be committed to the long haul, then we must appreciate the value of the incremental and commit ourselves to building brick by brick.

To have the right expectations of yourself means finding the balance between diligence, hard work and faith-suffused realism.

The Expectations of the Elders/Leaders

Tension in ministry is often caused when there is a mismatch between the expectations of your superior (whether that is a department head, a supervisor or a board of elders) and your own understanding of those expectations. The following would help:

- **A clear and detailed job description** – Although a job description cannot cover every expectation, it can be a good starting point. Generally, the more detailed it is, the better. For example, a part of the job description may read:

  - Responsible for pastoral care of those sick and in hospital

  Though it seems reasonable, this is actually very unclear unless it's expanded with more detail. Does it mean that you personally are supposed to visit the sick, or can you send someone else? Within what timeframe are you supposed to respond if you hear someone has been taken to the hospital? Immediately? Within 24 hours? 48 hours? Are you supposed to visit sick individuals who are at home? Are you expected to serve Communion to them, or prepare a devotion? Is there a prayer team that needs to be informed? It would be much better if this requirement were broken down to something more like:

- Responsible for pastoral care of those sick and in hospital:
  o By visiting those in the hospital within 24 hours of admission and contacting family
  o By visiting those sick at home at least once per month, and contacting them weekly by phone or e-mail
- If you cannot do those things because of other prior or unmovable commitments, ensure that another staff member can.

With this more-detailed description, you know exactly what is expected of you, and you and your superior could follow this up with a discussion of what exactly a hospital or home visit should look like. A person's background, prior church experience, personal preference, etc., all play into how that person understands the pastor's role in such situations, and you need to make sure that your understanding and theirs are the same, or negotiate it to something more workable if it seems unrealistic or unreasonable.

- **A discussion of what success looks like –** Beyond the bare bones of the job description, there are usually other expectations, which can be uncovered by a detailed discussion of what success looks like in a certain area. That may cover the "how" aspects in addition to the "what." For example, a job description might say, "Grow the youth ministry to 50 young people by November." The youth pastor might decide that putting up a skateboard ramp (cost: $3,000) in the church parking lot would be an ideal way of getting to such numbers, and before you know it, there are 75 skateboarders causing havoc in the church parking lot every Wednesday night. The elders are concerned now about liability issues, fielding complaints from neighbors about the noise, and questions from the treasurer about why the whole youth budget has been spent already. The "how" of the ministry should have been discussed.

If what the senior pastor had in mind was an in-house Bible study consisting of small groups totaling 50 young people, then that should have been specified. Success would have been clearly defined as "50 young people in small Bible study groups on Wednesday evenings, with a budget for curriculum not exceeding $300" – rather than simply a description of numerical growth. Without such specifics, you would have a very disgruntled youth pastor, who did what was asked ("I got 50 young people here") and a very unhappy senior pastor who wonders why the youth pastor didn't know what he wanted.

Being very specific at the outset avoids massive misunderstanding and disappointment later.

For the manager or supervisor, a method that could be employed to help with specifics would be the DR. GRAC method, which is primarily used as a tool for delegation but can easily be adapted for goal-setting and expectations. The acronym breaks down like this:

DR (Desired Results) – What exactly is the desired end product here?

G (Guidelines) – What are the parameters and rules around this?

R (Resources available?) What can be used in terms of facilities, finances and personnel?

A (Accountability) – What is the reporting supposed to look like? Do you check in with me? Do I send a written report? Do we have a weekly/monthly meeting?

C (Consequences) – What will result from either success or failure with this project? Promotion? Pay increase? Increased responsibility – or the opposite if it doesn't happen? Increased coaching and guidance perhaps?

Using DR. GRAC helps both parties be clear about what exactly is expected.

If the supervisor has prior experience with a similar project or situation, the supervisor can also inform the employee of the "chutes and ladders" – the potential traps to avoid, and the things that can accelerate or assist in a project's success. You can also use DR. GRAC successfully with volunteers.

- ◆ **A discussion of "unwritten assumptions"** – Even after the above two elements, there may still be more that is useful to know, often in terms of a church's or organization's culture, or simply "the way we do things around here." Generally those are things that are just "understood" or thought to be "common sense" and may not be specified in an employee or policy manual (though they should be). This can include things such as office hours, appropriate attire, what meetings you are expected to attend (even if you have no role) and so on. If you are able to meet with another employee who is a fairly recent hire, you may be able to ask what that staff member has learned about the organization's culture that isn't covered in a manual.

The Expectations of the Congregation

Sometimes a congregation has expectations of a pastor that – although they would never see the light of a job description are, for them, so obvious that they should not need to be mentioned. These "cultural" expectations can be deeply rooted, and offending against them could put your job in jeopardy.

In some congregations, to have a political affiliation other than the congregational mainstream might be a cause of contention (a Democrat among Republicans or vice versa). There might be certain unspoken assumptions about whether the pastor may or may not consume alcohol in certain circumstances, or what rating of movies it is acceptable for a pastor to view. Should the male pastor ever counsel a woman alone? Can the youth pastor drive a young girl home from the youth group? Can the church credit card be used to fill up your personal car if you are driving it to summer camp?

Especially in churches where a former pastor has experienced moral failure, there can be heightened sensitivity about such issues. Expectations regarding some of them could certainly be guessed at with common sense and wisdom, but the young pastor coming into a new congregation would do well to try and ascertain what those unwritten cultural assumptions are.

Additionally, if you are married, there may be certain expectations about the role or level of involvement of your spouse. Some churches have almost no expectations of a spouse beyond that the spouse attend church regularly like any normal member of the congregation. Other churches expect the spouse to have a very active role in the church, almost acting like an unpaid employee, and the churches imagine that by employing the pastor, they get the spouse thrown in for free. It is wise to ask what the level of involvement was for the former pastor's spouse. That might give you a clue to the likely expectations.

Many pastors entering ministry for the first time are at the young-family stage, and quite rightly expect that their spouse will play a primary and important role in raising the family. Knowing from experience how demanding that can be, it is good to ask whether your spouse would be expected to be at midweek or non-Sunday events, and to ascertain whether the church sees the spouse's involvement (or limited involvement) the same way you do.

The Whale and the Octopus

There are perhaps some types of congregation members that deserve a special mention. I call them the "whale and the octopus." These are not necessarily negative depictions. The "whales" (borrowing from Vegas terminology for high-rolling gamblers) are those who have a large financial investment in the church, either by virtue of their current high giving or their former generous donations. In the best case scenarios, such generosity comes with no strings attached and is simply a heartfelt commitment, expressed financially, to furthering the Kingdom of God through the local church. On the other end of the spectrum, though, generous givers may feel that because of the amount of their financial contribution, their concerns deserve special attention and compliance. Though they may not threaten it directly, often the implicit message may be, "If you don't do it the way I want, me and my money will be leaving this church."

How do you guard against that type of financial blackmail? I have always made it a policy to never know what any member of the congregation gives. I know many pastors follow a different approach and make specific, personal appeals to those who have greater financial capacity. I don't judge them for that, but I know that I would not feel comfortable doing that. I prefer that only the person who registers the giving in the church records knows what they give – and that person must be a person of extreme discretion and confidentiality.

As a person responsible for their spiritual care, and looking out for the good of the whole church, I want my counsel and approach to be unaffected by worrying about how a certain action or position would be received by these people, and whether there would be financial consequences.

Of course, any pastor considering a major transition in a church would be wise to consider the "stakeholders" – those who have a major investment in the church, but that is simply smart and honoring of those who have invested themselves into the church. Their investment may or may not have included very generous financial giving. Quite simply, there are those who care deeply about the church who may not have the means to be extremely generous financially, but whose opinions and counsel are just as valuable to you. Do not be driven by what will please the generous givers. Be driven by the revelation of the Spirit of God and by the godly counsel of those who love the church and (presumably) love you.

The "octopus" is someone who may have no official roles or titles or function within the church, but has tentacles in everything. Such individuals' value (and potential liability) to the church is that they are extremely well connected with diverse groups within the church. They are influential, and others seek their opinions and respond in a similar fashion. It would be wise for any new pastor to find out not only who the official "power brokers" (elders/deacons, etc.) are in the church, but also who the high influencers are. For example, there could be a former pastor in the church who has no official role but who is dearly loved and highly respected by the people.

When considering transitions or departures from "the way it has always been done," it would be wise to include such people in a type of "focus group." You should approach them and say something like, "There are some changes I'm thinking of making, and I know that you have experience and knowledge of this congregation. Would you mind me running them by you to see how you think that would play out?" Ideally the individuals would feel honored that you feel they are worth consulting, and be able to give you a good sense of how your move might play out, and what dangers or pitfalls could await you.

The law of unintended consequences means that whenever you make a change, it has "knock-on" effects that you would have found difficult to predict. Having wise counselors prior to the decision can help you spot potential trouble and can turn such people into strong advocates when a change is made.

Such people could form the basis of a type of "Leadership Advisory Team," though you should be careful that the group is not viewed as an alternative or rival team to your main advisors, whether that is a larger pastor/staff group or a board of elders, church council, etc. At best they would be a supplement, a grassroots, "ears to the ground" group who could assist you in predicting the consequences of change and being strong advocates of such change when it occurs, because they feel a sense of ownership and involvement.

God's Expectations

You would naturally expect that since the biblical standards for an elder are clearly set out in the Scriptures (1 Timothy 3:1-13 and Titus 1:5-9), they would be minimum standards for those of us honored with the title "pastor." They include:

1 Timothy 3:1-13

- Above reproach
- Married to just one spouse
- Temperate (not volatile)
- Self-controlled (emotionally stable and not given to rash action or words)
- Respectable
- Hospitable (simply being friendly and open toward others)
- Able to teach (able to handle the Word of God and pass it on with integrity)
- Not given to drunkenness (and, by implication, to any addiction or substance abuse)
- Not violent but gentle (both in action and words)
- Not quarrelsome (even when you know you are right!)
- Not a lover of money (this gets to motive for ministry)
- Good managers of their own family (stable home life with obedient children – though as the father of 4- and 7-year-olds, I am well aware that this is not 100% under my control!)
- Not a recent convert (must be grounded in the faith to avoid conceit/pride)
- Good reputation with outsiders

<u>Titus 1:5-9</u>:
- Blameless
- Having only one spouse
- Believing children who are not wild and disobedient
- Not overbearing (not lording it over others)
- Not quick-tempered
- Not given to drunkenness (addiction/substance abuse)
- Hospitable
- Loving what is good
- Self-controlled and upright
- Holy
- Disciplined
- Holding firmly to the truths of the faith to encourage others with sound doctrine, and refuting those who are heretical

Phew. That's quite a list, and honestly, none of us would probably score an A on all of them. We hope that we would at least qualify with a passing grade on most of them, and that for the ones that need work, the trajectory is in a positive direction.

Those are the givens.

More than this though, I think we need to consider what constitutes success in the eyes of God, and recognize that it may be very different than that which is normally acknowledged as success in society, or even Christian culture. The typical measures of success in church culture are numbers-driven. The most common questions pastors ask of each other at conferences have to do with attendance and the size of the budget. It's interesting that in the New Testament, the apostle Paul never mentions those areas when he's reporting on the churches he has planted. He is certainly interested in the quality of their faith, and that they have generous hearts, but church attendance and budgets don't seem to be that important to him.

Now, at a certain level, of course, numbers are important. Every person that comes to faith in Christ is a person who has been translated from the kingdom of darkness into the kingdom of light, and I would never want to underestimate the eternal value or significance of that. However, does success as a pastor necessarily mean that the church grows by huge numbers? Is growing the church to 1,000 members valuable to God? Would He not be equally – or perhaps more – pleased, for example, with a congregation of 100 that has planted nine other churches with 100 each in the last three years?

We should not be so naïve as to think that pastors cannot be ambitious, and honestly, that ambition is not always godly. Most of us enjoy the approval of our peers, and the standard markers for success are increasing Sunday attendance and an ever-growing budget. It would be refreshing if, instead, we placed an equal or greater value on depth of discipleship, sincerity of worship, generous giving (whether or not it meets budget), lives put back together by God, growth in love for God and neighbor... By the traditional markers of attendance and budget, a church packed full of unredeemed, unsaved, rich and generous pagans would be a great church! In the eyes of God it would be a failure.

In the final analysis, God calls us to be faithful, to discharge the duties of a pastor in the best way we can with the resources available to us. Faithfulness is our part. The results are up to Him. That does not justify passivity, poor planning or laziness (the Lord will bring who He wants). It should, though, make us realize that in the end, it is God who draws people, however wonderful our worship band and preaching are, and that the truly valuable result of transformed lives is His responsibility.

Someone once said that God is more concerned with what He can do in you, than what he can do through you, and you can be sure there is truth to that. The state of your own heart is of prime importance, and if envy, ambition, and neglect of family accompany your numerical success, you can be sure that things are not as God wants them to be.

In the economy of God, we may find that the humble missionary who has served in a barren mission field faithfully for 30 years, and has only seen two converts, may be wearing a larger crown in heaven than the mega-church pastor who has filled his auditorium with thousands. God knows our hearts. He calls us to be faithful.

GLYN NORMAN

CHAPTER 3:
TIME MANAGEMENT

One of the challenges a new pastor faces is that of time management – how to juggle the various responsibilities and infinite needs with a finite supply of time. Over the last few decades a raft of time-management techniques have been advanced[1], all of some value, but in the final analysis it is effectiveness and not mere efficiency that will move you toward success.

"Efficiency" merely means that you can do tasks more quickly. It says nothing about whether they are the things you should be doing. "Effectiveness" speaks to whether you are doing the right things in an efficient way, and it is more relevant for our purposes.

Efficiency tells us how to climb the ladder more quickly. Effectiveness makes sure the ladder is placed against the right building.

---

[1] For example: Franklin Covey Time Management Systems; Getting Things Done; The 4-Hour Workweek (Tim Ferriss), etc.

Effectiveness

So, how do we become more effective in ministry? The simple equation is to be doing the right things (effectiveness) in the right amount of time (efficiency).

The task of determining the right things is not always easy. Many competing demands and apparent priorities jostle for your attention. Stephen Covey[2] divides tasks into four quadrants. The vertical axis runs from non-important to important. The horizontal axis runs from urgent to non-urgent.

	URGENT	NOT URGENT
IMPORTANT	**Quadrant 1** Crisis Pressing issues Deadlines Meetings	**Quadrant 2** Preparation Planning Prevention Relationship building Personal development
NOT IMPORTANT	**Quadrant 3** Interruptions Some mail Popular activities	**Quadrant 4** Trivia Some phone calls Excessive TV/Games Time wasters

---

[2] Covey, Steven, The 7 Habits of Highly Effective People, Free Press, New York, NY, 1989

- ◆ Quadrant 1 might include things such as a phone call from an elder tell you that someone from the church has been admitted to the hospital. That is clearly both urgent and important.

- ◆ Quadrant 3 might be a person walking into your office with no particular agenda, just wishing to chat. You cannot ignore the person, and you must respond to the individual's presence, but it may not be that important.

- ◆ Quadrant 4 is the quadrant of waste, which might include aimless web surfing or playing computer games.

- ◆ Quadrant 2 is the ideal quadrant, which could involve things such as sermon series planning and so on.

The goal is to live above the line, so that the vast majority of your activities are spent on only that which is important. The more time you spend in Quadrant 2, the fewer items will become urgent, because you have already addressed many of them with preparatory work.

The sad reality is that many people spend most of their time in Quadrants 1 and 3, becoming burned out from the (apparent) urgency of everything before them. In order to recover from this burnout, they "veg" in Quadrant 4, which leads to less important work being done, increasing the likelihood of more time in Quadrants 1 and 3 … and so the spiral continues.

Priorities

There are two major cures to stop the spiral. One is to accurately identify our true priorities. If we have not identified the real priorities for the day or the week, our time will flow to whatever appears in front of us or to wherever our unfocussed attention drifts. Covey's book gives excellent advice on how to identify and manage priorities according to your true values, rather than the varying demands of your circumstances. I consider it a "must-read" for anyone wishing to grow in effectiveness.

Planning

The second cure is planning, both weekly and daily. Ask yourself these questions:

- If I were only able to accomplish one thing this week that would truly serve the goals of this church, what would it be?
- If I were only able to do one thing today, what should that be?

The answers to these simple questions should help ensure that, at a minimum, you are accomplishing the most important task for every day and the most important task for the whole week. That alone could massively increase your effectiveness.

Tips and Tools

Other than that, most of what would help are simple time-management practices, of which the following are a sample:

- Only check and answer e-mail twice per day,

at 11 a.m. and 3 p.m.[3]

Many of us are e-mail junkies, and we go to our Inbox to get our "hit" multiple times a day. It's not unlike a rat in an experiment constantly pushing a lever to get a pleasurable sensation. There's a psychological payoff to receiving e-mail – I am important; people wish to communicate with me; I cannot afford to be out of touch – but there is also a cost: Each time you stop what you are doing to check e-mail, you lose not only the time you spend doing that but also the time it takes for you to refocus on your prior task. That can easily cost an hour or more per day, since experts estimate that this act of refocusing can take 15 minutes to get back up to your former speed and level of concentration.

If you work in an environment where quick response to e-mail is expected, then you may need to retrain your colleagues to your new method of working. Tim Ferriss suggests that you create an auto-responder that checks your e-mail every 15 minutes or so and sends a reply along the following lines: "I am currently seeking to be more efficient by only checking e-mail twice per day. If your question requires a more immediate response, please call me on my cellphone. Otherwise, I will try to respond promptly after those set times."

This auto-response filters those questions

---

[3] See Tim Ferriss' excellent book, <u>The 4-Hour Workweek</u>, (Crown Publishers, New York, NY, 2007) to understand how beneficial this can be.

that are truly important and urgent from those that can be answered at a more optimal time for you. A word of caution: This practice may or may not be acceptable in your environment. Be wise.

◆ Batch similar tasks together.

Our mind tends to get in certain ruts, and you can use that to your advantage. Bearing in mind the loss of time that comes from switching tasks and refocusing, try to batch similar tasks together. If you are dealing with your credit-card receipts and invoices, do them all together. Your mind will be in "math mode," and you'll accomplish the task much quicker than if you switch from sermon preparation to credit-card receipts to answering an email about a pastoral need, to invoices, and so on. Even answering e-mail twice per day is a batch method, which will encourage you to be more "ruthless" in dealing with what comes in.[4]

◆ Determine your most productive times of the day/week and allocate accordingly.

For myself, my creative work tends to happen best in the mornings, so that is time I try to set aside for writing, sermon preparation, etc. This means that if possible, I try to set appointments with people for the

---

[4] Check out Merlin Mann's productivity website, 43folders.com for tips on how to reduce your e-mail inbox to zero consistently.

afternoon, when interactivity with people is more effective at keeping me alert than staring at a computer screen. Work out the rhythm of your week. When are you most fresh? When do you feel most tired? Allocate routine, low-concentration-required tasks to the tired times and the most demanding tasks to your higher-energy times.

• Break down mammoth tasks into smaller steps.

Sometimes projects are so huge that we have an inner psychological urge to not deal with them. The problem is that this mammoth project is always at the back of our mind, slowly draining us. Projects become much more manageable if we break them down into smaller, more achievable steps. As the saying goes: How do you eat an elephant? One bite at a time. Take your elephant project and break it down into smaller tasks. You will feel a much greater sense of progress in achieving some of the smaller tasks, and it will make the whole project appear more achievable. Ask yourself questions such as:

- What can I do this week to move this project further along?
- What goals can I identify that will get me closer? (Use S.M.A.R.T. goals – Specific, Measurable, Attainable, Realistic, Timely.)

♦ Retrain your interrupters.

It is part of the pastoral makeup that we wish to be available and helpful, but the simple fact is that people can make unrealistic and unreasonable demands upon your time. If you give in to them, then you are basically rewarding such behavior and encouraging it to continue. Of course, there will always be the genuine crisis that requires an immediate response, but often, someone else's sense of priority may not match yours. Their sudden sense of urgency need not necessarily become your crisis.

I read of a pastor who sometimes received calls from a woman who was experiencing what she considered to be a marital crisis, and who demanded immediate intervention and counseling. When the pastor asked the nature of the problem, and then asked how long it had been going on, the person replied, "About a year." A problem that has been going on for a year is not an immediate crisis. In that case, the pastor wisely said that he was currently preparing the sermon for Sunday, and that if this was a genuine crisis needing his immediate intervention, then he would gladly sacrifice that preparation time to help, but in this case, could it wait until Monday? The caller grudgingly admitted that it could.

The re-training can also extend to interruptions on your day off. Some people do not realize that a pastor needs genuine time to be off-duty (barring emergencies, such as a death in the family) and that if he is to remain sharp, focused and renewed, his "down time" is essential. It is worth informing your congregation of your policy. My congregation knows that I take Fridays and Saturdays off, and generally is kind enough not to disturb me on those days. I've also let it be known that Wednesdays are usually my sermon preparation day, and so people are cautious about interrupting that time, too. The patterns you set early on in ministry will be the ones that reward you – or haunt you, if you choose unwisely.

Your time is a precious and limited resource, and once it's lost, it can never be regained. Tact may be required to inform your congregation, and even other staff members, of your protected times, but the reward in terms of increased productivity is immense. Naturally, unless you are the senior pastor (and perhaps even then, if you have a very involved elder board), you may need to gain permission for such policies of time protection.

CHAPTER 4:
WORKING WITH VOLUNTEERS

The Great Resource

As a pastor first starting out in ministry, with a normal and understandable desire to impress, you will want to do much of the work of ministry yourself. However, it will soon become apparent that there is a gap between the work that is needed for the advancement of the Kingdom of God, and the resources you personally have available in terms of your own time and energy.

That is where an important philosophy of ministry concept comes in: the priesthood of all believers . This is attested by many New Testament passages, such as 1 Peter 2:9, which says:

But you are a chosen people, a royal priesthood, a holy nation, a people belonging to God, that you may declare the praises of him who called you out of darkness into his wonderful light.

Added to that are the various passages about spiritual gifts, such as 1 Corinthians 12, Romans 12 and Ephesians 4, which have the inherent implication that if believers have gifts, they should use them for the building up of the church in some way. In fact, Ephesians 4:11-13 is a direct challenge to the way in which most of us view ministry:

It was he who gave some to be apostles, some to be prophets, some to be evangelists, and some to be pastors and teachers, to prepare God's people for works of service, so that the body of Christ may be built up until we all reach unity in the faith and in the knowledge of the Son of God and become mature, attaining to the whole measure of the fullness of Christ.

In seminary or Bible college, we are trained to do the work of ministry, and of course, there are some roles that we are naturally expected to fill. However, note the emphasis here: God has given apostles, prophets, evangelists, pastors and teachers to prepare God's people for works of service – not to do the all the work of ministry themselves. That means a significant part of a pastor's role is to train and equip others for ministry.

This is the great resource: gifted, willing volunteers just waiting to be invited to join you in God's work. Sadly, it is often the great untapped resource, with an implicit clergy/laity divide still existing and with the vast majority of work still being done by the paid pastoral staff.

There are a number of problems with that approach. First, if that is your view, then your effectiveness is limited to what you, and you alone, can accomplish. However passionate, enthusiastic and energetic you are, your week only contains 168 hours, the same as everyone else's. Second, if you restrict all ministry to yourself, your susceptibility to burnout is dramatically increased, because the success of the ministry is even more directly related to your personal efforts. Third, this is not a scalable model. In other words, although you might competently do most of the pastoral work for a church of 100-200 people, if by God's grace the church grows, you will find that your resources are quickly outstripped by the needs of the congregation. Fourth, you are denying people the fulfillment and joy that comes from expressing the gifts that God has given them, and discovering what it means to be an instrument in the Redeemer's hands.

My favorite analogy for this untapped resource is the following question: If a house is on fire and you have a bucket of water in your hands, are you going to throw the water at the house or over the 10 sleeping firemen by the side of the road? In your church, you have many "sleeping firemen" just waiting to be "awoken" to the many ministry opportunities that await them, if only they were invited to participate.

Equipping Volunteers

So what does that mean for you as you enter ministry?

1. Teach or demonstrate your belief in the priesthood of all believers. If you say you believe in it but do all the work of ministry yourself, then people will not believe you.

2. Encourage all church members to discover their spiritual gifts. Make sure each person is aware that God has given a gift that can be

used to build up the church and advance the Kingdom. Help your members discover what their gifts are. Teach on them, hold seminars or workshops, direct people to online resources (simply do a web search for "spiritual gifts test," and you will find a number of free resources available). In my first church, where I became a Christian at age 20, the pastor, John Bishop, taught on spiritual gifts in the Sunday evening service for a year! After being a Christian for a year, I was ripe for getting my hands dirty in ministry – and that's the next step.

3. Give people opportunities to try ministry. After about a year of being a Christian, John Bishop invited me to help lead a small group with him and his wife, Lisa. Soon after, I was invited to be part of the evangelism team, to try my hand at leading worship and children's ministry, and finally was offered the opportunity to preach one-third of a sermon, together with two other young men in the church. That progressed to half a sermon (the first half … I'm thinking John wanted the opportunity to repair the damage if I went heretical on him ☺), and finally to a whole sermon on my own. Such exposure to a wide range of ministry opportunities gave me ample opportunity to discover how God had gifted me (preaching and teaching) and in what areas He hadn't (children's ministry). Try to build in evaluation, so that your volunteers can hone and develop their skills. Advise them of that beforehand, so they know to

expect it. "Let's plan on meeting after you preach and talk together about how it went" is better than you calling a surprise meeting, with them concluding that they must have messed up.

4. Develop a mindset of inclusion. Before every ministry activity, ask yourself, "Who can I include in this?" If you are about to visit someone in the hospital, think about who could come with you, watch what you do and say, and perhaps take part – maybe praying for the person at the end of the visit. With those steps you will multiply ministry exponentially beyond what you alone could accomplish.

5. Devolve ministry to the "lowest" possible level. What I mean by that is try to remove the idea that ministry is only "proper" if it is done by a paid staff member, preferably a pastor. Ideally, with the given example of a hospital visit, I would wish that a person's small group would be the ones rallying round and offering support and care. They actually do life with the person and know and his or her needs very well. They are better placed to offer genuine care than a pastor who may not know the person very well and who swings by for a 15-minute hospital visit. Depending on your denomination rules or church practice, you may want to authorize non-clergy to distribute Communion, pray for the sick, preach, lead Bible studies etc.

A word of caution though: Make sure that your board/elders are aware of your strategy and agree on the appropriate parameters. They may be all in favor of you training others to preach but would perhaps not like it if you were absent from the pulpit three weeks out of four, to allow opportunity for your "trainees."

The Currency of Appreciation

Volunteers are, by definition, unpaid helpers. That means the common forms of motivation available in the typical workplace (pay raises, promotions, etc.) are unavailable to you. What you do have, potentially in abundance, is appreciation. I cannot tell you how incredibly important it is that you appreciate your volunteers. That can range from an informal "Thanks so much for helping out" comment to a more formal appreciation dinner or event. Whatever you choose to do, make sure your volunteers know that their contribution is noticed and deeply appreciated.

If you can, try to write a few thank-you cards every week to people who are making a contribution. It may take just a few minutes for you to do, but what it gains you in terms of loyalty, and a person's sustained commitment, is inestimable. We often under-appreciate the power of our appreciation. On Sundays when I am not preaching, I sometimes wander around the children's classrooms and thank the workers for serving. It always amazes me how much that (seemingly) little gesture is appreciated. The last thing you want is for people to feel taken for granted, so do whatever you can to let them know how much you value them and what they do.

CHAPTER 5:
PREACHING

There is so much good advice, and there are so many excellent resources in circulation, not to mention the seminary training you received, that all I can hope to offer here are a few practical pointers that may not have been mentioned, or at least, sufficiently emphasized, elsewhere.

Preaching is an awesome and holy responsibility. When you preach, you have the opportunity to shape people's minds regarding how they think about God, each other and the world, and the potential to influence their behavior in life-changing ways. For most pastors, it is the most direct form of influence on the congregation that you have.

Consider, though, that with the average sermon lasting about 30 minutes, you have only 26 hours at your disposal over the course of a year – a little more than one 24-hour-day preaching marathon! Having such limited time and such incredible potential suggests that we should treat this holy task with immense respect.

Preparation

For that reason, I am a firm believer in protecting sermon preparation time. If you have experience in preaching, you will probably know how much time it takes you to prepare a decent sermon. That can vary enormously. Some preachers can crack out a top sermon in four hours; others struggle to complete it in 25 hours.

Make sure that the time you devote to sermon preparation is protected. Either create an environment where it is known that this is sacred time that should not be interrupted, or go somewhere where it is difficult for someone to reach you. For some pastors, there is a more immediate gratification that comes from helping someone with a pastoral need, so they would gladly drop their sermon preparation to help – but that is at a cost to the whole congregation if they don't recapture that time elsewhere. Is this 30-minute unscheduled interruption worth the trade of producing an inferior sermon for potentially hundreds or even thousands of your congregation on Sunday? If not, then attempt to kindly and tactfully reschedule.

In terms of actual preparation, individuals vary so vastly in their style and personality that it would be foolishness to advocate any particular method. However, in my own experience, the following components have proved useful in my sermon preparation.

I find it important to get myself in the right frame of mind. Sometimes that is achieved through prayer; sometimes I'm already there, and sometimes I just need to start and trust that God will get me there quickly. In the ideal world, our sermons would flow from souls that are full of God and overflowing with the fruit of our own study and relationship with God. At the other end of the spectrum, we may sometimes approach the Bible like burglars, just looking to raid it for a quick prize that will preach. In most of our cases, we're probably somewhere nearer the middle of that line, but the goal should always be to edge toward the former reality rather than the latter. For me, the preparation and the final sermon writing need to have some space between them. I need time for the fruits of my study to percolate in my mind, so that when the time comes for my final draft, I have a good sense of what to cut and what to include. There may be an illustration I read and discarded, but which keeps coming back to me. The percolation time allows me to realize that this illustration grabbed me somehow, and it might also have a similar effect on the congregation.

One danger for us, if our preaching preparation time is curtailed, is that we revert back to old, tried and trusted messages (if we have them) or simply bang on about our favorite themes. You may get away with that occasionally, but it does not produce the balanced diet that a congregation needs.

A Balanced Approach

Ideally, if you have a regular preaching calendar, try to create a balanced approach. What that means in your particular environment may vary. For some churches, the primary preaching approach is topical. For others, it may be preaching expositionally through a book of the Bible. In any case, be sure that there is balance, perhaps by asking yourself the following questions:

- Is there a mix of Old Testament and New Testament in my preaching?

- Am I focusing just on epistles and writings of Paul, and neglecting the gospels?

- Whatever my subject, is the congregation learning more about Jesus?

- Is there a balance of exhortation and grace, or am I just always calling the congregation to a higher standard without allowing room for failure, growth and grace?

- Am I reactive, preaching just what the church "needs to hear right now"?

- Am I demonstrating how the Bible applies to everyday life, or focusing too much on academic doctrine?

- Am I assuming that everyone in the room is a Christian, or am I being sure to explain concepts to those who may not be well grounded or who may be very new to the church?

- In my preaching, is there a mix of a call to conversion and a call to deeper discipleship?

- Am I focusing on one demographic too much at the expense of others, e.g., young families, or single professionals?

My Method

I offer this description of my method purely as an example and not in any attempt to be prescriptive. You may have your own sermon preparation system that works perfectly well for you. That's fine, but on the off-chance that something here may help …

1. Prayer and pre-sermon preparation

    At the very least I want to spend some time getting my own heart right before I presume to be a speaking vessel for the Almighty God. Confession and offering myself to God for his service are components of that time. I may get "in the mood" for writing a sermon. I may not. Sometimes it is when I have begun the preparation (not before) that I start to feel inspired.

2. Raw text and ideas

    Assuming that I am preaching from a passage without any hidden agenda, what I first want to do is the normal work of reading and understanding the Bible text, without referring to any commentaries. I want to make sure I understand what the text says rather than what I want it to say. The normal process of hermeneutics/context, etc., takes place here. As I read, I start to write ideas on a blank sheet of paper. I use a mind-map type of diagram such as this:

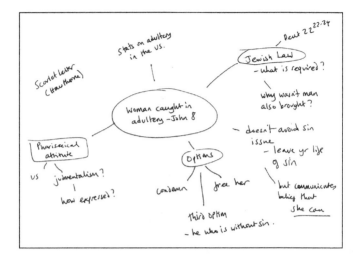

Using that type of diagram means I am not forced to be linear. As an idea or theme from the text occurs to me, I can simply jot it down somewhere. At this point, I do not need to connect it or work out where in the flow it fits best. If a quote or movie clip that might be relevant occurs to me, I just throw it in there. I can draw connecting lines, erase it (I do this in pencil) and move it somewhere else, put a number next to it – whatever I like.

At this point, I'm simply in a "capturing information" phase. I find that at that 30,000-feet level, broad ideas occur to me that may not pop up once I am digging into the theological details contained in a commentary. For example, I was preparing a sermon on wisdom, and the idea popped in my head, "What 'wisdom' have I heard that was ridiculous?" and I remembered my mother telling me that if I watched too much TV, my eyes would go square. The note "Mother-TV-Eyes Square" made it onto the mind-map, and I started the sermon asking people in the congregation what so-called wisdom they had received that turned out to be completely untrue. It made for an engaging and amusing start to the message.

3. Commentaries

After the work with the raw text has been done, I dig into the commentaries. For me, that is fun. I realize that this is not true for everyone. At the very least I want to make sure my basic understanding of a passage is sound and that what the commentators are saying is along the same lines. If it isn't, then some serious re-working may be required. If I am saying something about the text that no one else has ever said, I may be veering toward heresy. Either that, or I am particularly gifted ... but probably heretical! If the commentaries suggest further thoughts, then I add those to the mind-map. I may use online or printed resources for this stage (see the Resources section for more guidance).

4. Application

Scripture needs to be applied. People need to understand how the truths can affect their everyday life.

In my own preparation, I try to imagine myself sitting around a kitchen table having a conversation with a group of people. There may be a single mother with three small children, a businessman, a college student, a retired homemaker, a young professional who is not a Christian and is checking out the church for the first time (add more characters appropriate to your congregation). I ask myself whether what I'm writing would make sense to those people? For example, if my solution to worry is to spend three hours a day in prayer and Scripture reading (since I have great control over my own time), thinking about that group would make me realize that it would be a completely impractical solution for the young mother, and I might need to think of ways of applying the point differently.

I want to be cautious about not giving my particular application the weight of biblical authority unless it is truly warranted. For example, I might be preaching on "Honor your father and mother" and make the statement, "It is dishonoring to put your aged father or mother in a nursing home." That is going beyond what the text says. I cannot, and should not, place such authority on my particular interpretation of a command. In some circumstances it may be completely honoring to make that decision in order to ensure that aged parents receive the best care available. For other commands, such as the command to "Forgive others as Christ forgave you," I am on much safer ground to say that you must forgive.

5. Illustrations

Illustrations can be key to helping a congregation understand a point more deeply or grasping its relevance.

I learned in my younger days that an illustration can be too good. An illustration can be so vivid and memorable that people will not take away anything else from the sermon – and the illustration may have been intended to illumine a minor point. I once told three illustrations in 5 minutes that involved death, vomit and blood. They were very vivid and memorable, but that's all people could think about. The main points of my message were obliterated by my Technicolor gore! Try to ensure that your illustration makes your point clearer rather than completely eclipsing it.

Generally, I try to use illustrations from my own life and experience rather than ones found online, though they can sometimes be very useful.

6. Time

After I have done the prep work, I usually try to leave a day or two before I write the final script. That allows the ideas to ferment, and I find that the ones that have stayed with me are the ones that are most likely to connect with the congregation. My theory is that if I can't forget them, then probably the congregation will find them somewhat memorable. When I come back to the mind-map, I can usually see what flow or order the points should follow and perceive the natural pathways of the message. From that point, it usually takes me about two hours to write the message in full.

7. Brevity

I usually aim to preach for about 30-40 minutes. The expectation of the church may be different, and that is useful to clarify. One caution I have for young or relatively inexperienced preachers is this: Don't try to preach it all at once. You may have four or five sermons bubbling inside you, but please only give the congregation one at a time. Stick to the main thrust of the one message and don't deviate from it. Sometimes if a preacher only preaches occasionally, he feels the temptation to make the most of it and attempts to say everything that can be said about the topic. That can make the congregation overwhelmed, as though they are trying to drink from a firehouse. If, in your preparation, you sense that you are trying to preach two messages, then separate them out, and do each one well, rather than preaching a confusing mega-message. Remember, preaching is incremental. You do not need to say "all that can be said" in just one message. Also remember that preaching is different from writing a paper. Every point does not need to be proved beyond exhaustion. Sometimes we can over-justify our positions and leave the congregation antsy, wishing that we would just move on, because they already "get it," and additional justification becomes superfluous.

Resources

Jesus promised that His Holy Spirit would lead us into all truth and this generous gift must be considered a precious resource.

Different translations of the Bible can sometimes add a different perspective, but make sure they are decent translations, rather than paraphrases.

Many excellent commentary sets are available, but if I could only choose three, these are what I would choose:

- **Expositor's Bible Commentary** (Frank E. Gaebelein, general editor), 12 volumes – my top choice. It offers a great balance between scholarly interpretation and relevant application.
- **NIV Application Commentary** – As the name suggests, this does a great job of revealing what issues were current then, what the bridging concepts are, and what application it has for today.
- **Word Biblical Commentary** – This is the most hardcore and the most technical of all the commentaries. Mostly I skip the Form/Structure/Setting Sections, and read only the Comment and Explanation sections. You are unlikely to need anything more detailed than that.

For background and more-detailed topical exploration of Bible issues, there is a series called Dictionary of …, published by IVP. These include:

+ Dictionary of the Old Testament Pentateuch
+ Dictionary of the Old Testament Historical Books
+ Dictionary of the Old Testament Wisdom, Poetry and Writings
+ Dictionary of New Testament Background
+ Dictionary of Jesus and the Gospels
+ Dictionary of Paul and His Letters
+ Dictionary of the Later New Testament and Its Development

If you ever want to know what the Pentateuch says about sacrifice, what Jesus says about hell, or what Paul says about Communion, those dictionaries are a wonderful resource which gathers that all together.

If you do not have access to those commentaries (they can be expensive), then some good, free online resources are also available:

+ **www.soniclight.com** Click the Study Notes section and navigate to the passage you are studying. Dr Thomas L. Constable is a reliable, conservative evangelical scholar.
+ **www.textweek.com** Click the Scripture Index link and navigate to the relevant passage. This site is unique in that it also offers suggestions for movie clips or art that would relate to that topic or passage (Use Movie Index or Art Index for those). It offers different Bible translations of the passage, ancient commentaries from the early church

fathers, later commentaries from the likes of Martin Luther, John Calvin, Matthew Henry and the like, and even recent sermons and academic papers, drama, clip art, graphics, hymns and music that relate to the passage in question.

◆ **www.preachingtoday.com** This site requires an annual subscription (recently $79) but allows you a 30-day free access trial. It is a treasure trove for illustrations (more than 11,000) and is searchable either by topic or Bible passage. You can also specify the nature of the illustrations you desire (e.g., funny, serious).

◆ **www.sermonspice.com** A site with a great collection of videos to enhance your sermon, it's themed, and with special holiday focus videos (e.g., Thanksgiving, Veteran's Day, etc.) The videos are downloadable in various formats, and usually less than $20 each.

◆ **www.biblegateway.com** This has a passage lookup, keyword search and topical index, for those messages for which you wish to get an overview of what the Bible says about a certain issue.

Caution

A last word of caution: Beware of using the bully pulpit. There may be times in the life of the church when you suspect, or know, that certain people or groups are against you. It can be tempting to use your uninterrupted 30 minutes of preaching time to "set a few things straight." Unless that is done wisely, in an attempt to challenge clear sin, it will almost always backfire. To preach against gossip is one thing; to preach a message about "God not living in buildings made by human hands" when you know the building committee is pushing you to approve a new building project would be an abuse. If you are not careful, your preaching can become reactive, essentially becoming a passive-aggressive attack on those who disagree with you.

If you find yourself tempted to go down that path, admit your motives to yourself (and preferably a trusted friend/counselor outside your current situation), and rather than confront issues in that way, use a more biblical approach along the lines of Matthew 18, rather than taking sermonic sideswipes at your detractors. (See the "Dealing With Conflict" section)

CHAPTER 6:
COUNSELING

Most pastors are drawn to ministry because of the potential to help people. The forms in which that can happen are varied, and we will naturally be better at some than others. Whatever your strength, it is highly likely that at some point someone will come to you for counsel. I hope the following will prove helpful as you explore this area of ministry.

Time Availability and Emotional Reserves

You will have to decide for yourself (unless it is decided for you) how much of your time can be devoted to meeting with members of the congregation one-on-one in a counseling-type environment. Too little, and you risk being viewed as distant and lacking in compassion and shepherd-type care for the flock. Too much, and you will severely restrict the time you have available for other areas of ministry.

It is important to have good boundaries, which will

depend on your psychological makeup. You may only be able to handle one counseling appointment per week. You might have such deep empathy that you carry the person's problems with you and find them hard to shake off emotionally. To enter deeply into another person's pain may be so costly for you emotionally that you will need to monitor carefully how much of that you can do. Another pastor, with different wiring, may be able to handle multiple intense appointments without thinking about those issues outside of work. For professional counselors and therapists that is pretty much an essential skill or disposition. Be aware of how counseling appointments affect you.

To do that well requires emotional self-awareness. Some ministry tasks are not emotionally draining. For me, studying in preparation for a sermon is not an emotionally demanding task. Other ministry tasks, however, are very emotionally demanding. I remember performing a funeral and being confronted with the scene of the bereft wife weeping and clutching onto the casket of her deceased husband. That was very emotionally distressing for me, as I felt the weight of her grief. I had planned to go back to the office after the funeral, but as I was driving away, I realized that I was pretty much drained and needed some time to emotionally recover from the intensity of that situation before I would be useful for any other ministry task. Being aware of your reaction to counseling situations is important for maintaining good boundaries.

Codependency

Another danger is that of codependency, usually

defined as "needing to be needed." To be able to help another person, to hear that you are making a difference, giving clarity, bringing healing – those things can be intoxicating. "Someone came and talked to me, and their world is better as a result!" If we are not careful, we can enjoy the validation of that feeling too much, and our need to be a counselor may outweigh a person's need for counseling. We may, either deliberately or subconsciously, continue the counseling arrangement longer than we should, because we enjoy the feeling of helping someone.

It is worth remembering that our goal is to move people to dependency on Christ, not on us as their pastor. My general rule of thumb is that I will counsel people perhaps two or three times. If their issue is so complex that it requires more time than that, then I should refer them to a professional. If I find myself looking forward to the counseling appointment, then I should seriously consider whose needs are being met by the meeting. Absolute honestly may compel me to admit that it is my sense of fulfillment or usefulness that is driving me, and I must have integrity enough to back away.

You Are Not the Messiah

For some pastors, the challenge of helping people who are struggling with personal issues becomes almost a personal challenge. "Others may have failed them, but I will be the one that brings them to a breakthrough." Be careful that you are not developing a Messiah-type complex, believing that you and your counsel are the answer to their problems. The danger in that, apart from them becoming too dependent on you, is that you may not realize when you are out of your depth. Your desire to help may cloud your judgment and hinder you from understanding when the issues require professional counseling or psychological help. If a person tells you that many others have tried to help before but failed, and the person is convinced that you will be the one who can truly help, be very wary. It plays into our natural desire to be helpful, and may feed our ego, but the likelihood is that the person knows what you like to hear and is telling you that as a form of emotional manipulation. It is hard to maintain appropriate boundaries if you are so manipulated. For myself, I usually tell people at the outset that I am a "short-term counselor" and that I usually meet with people for a maximum of three sessions. If I cannot help them within that time period, then the likelihood is that they would be better served by going to a professional counselor or joining a small group within a ministry like Celebrate Recovery. I couch all this within the framework of wanting the best care for them, and so far, everyone has understood and been receptive.

The Issue May Not Be Purely Spiritual

A last warning, which may sound strange, is that we must be careful not to assume that all problems are spiritual and/or psychological. Since we are pastors, we may quite rightly assume that we are well placed to deal with spiritual issues, and it is tempting to view all issues through that lens. As someone once said, "If you are a hammer, every problem looks like a nail." Although some issues may be rooted in a spiritual element, it could also be that a person may have a chemical imbalance in the brain. Let's not be so spiritually focused that we feel it is "ungodly" or "unspiritual" to recommend that the person see a doctor for tests. Some depression and other issues are chemical in nature, and outside of miraculous healing, it is unlikely that counsel or prayer alone will fix the problem.

Remember that the person reaching a state of health is the paramount concern, and that may involve including other professionals, be they trained counselors or medical personnel. Sometimes healing will come through a combination of wise counsel from a pastor leading a person to spiritual truth, and correct medication. It is not lacking faith to look at the issue from all angles.

Be Aware of Your Own Emotions

The counseling situation can become an intimate one. A person can be sharing deep secrets and entrusting them to you. The danger is acute when the person you are counseling is of the opposite gender. I think most men desire to rescue, to be "the knight in shining armor," and that desire, coupled with the intimacy of the counseling situation, can lead to an emotional closeness that is fraught with danger.

For example, in many situations in which is in a difficult relational situation with her husband, what she finds in you is a compassionate, intelligent man who is deeply interested in her problems. The potential for danger and confusion is obvious. Again, only radical honesty will save you here.

Your spouse can be your greatest ally. Enlist her help and tell her if mixed feelings may be developing, and then exit yourself from the counseling relationship as soon as possible. If you feel this is something you cannot tell your spouse, that in itself is the surest indicator that you should! Ideally, you and your spouse should set some ground rules before ever getting into such a situation. You could agree that if ever such a situation occurs, that you will tell her early on. She will agree not to hit you ☺, and to help you resolve the situation. Knowing that this can occur, and setting up a safety mechanism in advance to deal with it, is wise protection. An awkward and difficult conversation beforehand which helps avoid an incident is far better than a devastating conversation after something immoral has happened.

If there is something you feel you need to keep secret from your spouse, then alarm bells should be ringing. In my case, I am blessed with a wife who has the gift of discernment with people, and she will tell me if her "radar" is alerted by someone. Usually this sense comes without specific knowledge of why she feels uncomfortable about this person, but to me, that is warning enough to keep my distance.

If you are not married, then confide in an accountability partner or another pastor that you trust, and again, plan an exit from the counseling relationship. Having a team of qualified female counselors (or developing one) in the church gives you an easy referral opportunity.

Never tell individuals you are counseling that you may be developing feelings for them. That opens the door to them telling you how they feel about you – and disaster is knocking at your door. Simply explain that you believe you are not the person best placed to help them, and because their wellbeing is your primary concern, you wish to refer them to someone you see as better qualified, more experienced, etc.

You may think of yourself as spiritual and professional, and such things could not happen to you, but the reality is that even among counseling professionals who are trained to notice such things happening (transference), the rate of abuse is high. The data in one study showed that 12.1% of psychologists reported having sex with a client. (http://kspope.com/sexiss/sexencyc.php)

A 1988 survey in Leadership magazine reported that:

- Nearly one in four pastors admitted doing something "sexually inappropriate" with someone who was not their spouse;
- One in five pastors confessed to sexual misconduct of some kind;
- One in eight admitting adultery; and
- Only four in 100 were found out by their local church.

The statistics are more startling when the potential for multiple affairs is considered. Staheli says, "people who have affairs are likely to have more than one, especially men … About 25% of men and 15% of women who have affairs have four or more [affairs]." (http://www.ministryhealth.net/mh_articles/294_aff air_ proof_pastorate.html)

We are all vulnerable to such temptations, and perhaps most vulnerable of all when we think this is something that could not happen to us. Many pastors work in demanding situations that can be emotionally draining. When an attractive person who looks up to us offers us emotional support, and physical affection, it can be hard to resist. We need to be aware of our needs and make sure that those legitimate emotional needs are not met in an illegitimate way. Wise self-care is the first safeguard against such a failure. (See the Self-Care section.)

Simple, practical boundaries can also help. Some pastors never counsel a woman alone, but insist on another person always being present. Some never counsel a woman behind closed doors, but insist on meeting in a public place where others can clearly see them, or in a room with a window so others can see that nothing inappropriate is taking place. In today's litigious society, it is wise for the pastor, mindful of his own protection, to be in a situation in which it is easy to refute any claim of sexual harassment or inappropriateness. If you have such precautions in place, but are tempted to make an exception for a certain person, that should be warning enough that this is not a person you should counsel. People are harmed, families are wrecked and ministries ruined by pastors not being careful in this area. Be warned and be wise.

CHAPTER 7:
SELF-CARE

Burnout

The statistics of pastoral burnout in America are frightening. The New York Times (August 1, 2010) reports that: "Members of the clergy now suffer from obesity, hypertension and depression at rates higher than most Americans. In the last decade, their use of antidepressants has risen, while their life expectancy has fallen. Many would change jobs if they could."

* According to Daniel Sherman5, who has collated these statistics, this is the current landscape:13% of active pastors are divorced.
* 23% have been fired or pressured to resign at least once in their careers.
* 25% don't know where to turn when they have a family or personal conflict or issue.
* 25% of pastors' wives see their husband's

---

5 See Daniel Sherman's excellent website:
http://www.pastorburnout.com and his Pastor Burnout Workbook.

work schedule as a source of conflict.

* 33% felt burned out within their first five years of ministry.
* 33% say that being in ministry is an outright hazard to their family.
* 40% of pastors and 47% of spouses are suffering from burnout, frantic schedules, and/or unrealistic expectations.
* 45% of pastors' wives say the greatest danger to them and their family is physical, emotional, mental, and spiritual burnout.
* 45% of pastors say that they've experienced depression or burnout to the extent that they needed to take a leave of absence from ministry.
* 50% feel unable to meet the needs of the job.
* 52% of pastors say they and their spouses believe that being in pastoral ministry is hazardous to their family's well-being and health.
* 56% of pastors' wives say that they have no close friends.
* 57% would leave the pastorate if they had somewhere else to go or some other vocation they could do.
* 70% don't have any close friends.
* 75% report severe stress causing anguish, worry, bewilderment, anger, depression, fear, and alienation.
* 80% of pastors say they have insufficient time with their spouse.
* 80% believe that pastoral ministry affects their families negatively.
* 90% feel unqualified or poorly prepared for

ministry.
- 90% work more than 50 hours a week.
- 94% feel under pressure to have a perfect family.
- 1,500 pastors leave their ministries each month because of burnout, conflict, or moral failure.
- Doctors, lawyers and clergy have the most problems with drug abuse, alcoholism and suicide.

Clearly this is a different picture than most of our congregations imagine. Jokes about only working one day a week are diametrically opposite in reality to the stress and pressure many pastors feel.

Though great resources are available for pastors who have reached that point, surely our better approach is to defend against burnout in the first place. If you are experiencing symptoms that suggest burnout6, radical action may be required to get you to a place of health again. Let's consider some categories.

Emotional Self-Care

Of all the areas in which a pastor is vulnerable, I believe emotional burnout places at the top of the list. The diverse nature of the job requires emotional flexibility, which comes at a price. One moment you may be sitting in a budget meeting with an irascible committee member, butting heads as you work hard to convince him of the legitimacy of your planned ministry expenses for the next year. Thirty minutes later you could be counseling a bereaved widow who

---

6 http://www.pastorburnout.com/symptoms-of-burnout.html

just lost her husband of 50 years. You have had to move from "hard-headed persuasive number cruncher" to "compassionate friend in a time of need" in a few short minutes. That takes a toll emotionally.

For pastors who do a lot of counseling, the effect of this varies. If you are a person, like many professional counselors, who can leave it all behind at the end of the day, then probably it will not exact a great price from you. However, if you feel deeply, and carry someone's pain home with you (a problem for those with deep empathy), then it will have a cost.

Compounding that can be the sense that you are never off-duty. If congregation members see you in the supermarket on a Saturday, to them you are still Pastor X, and it surely wouldn't hurt for them to tell you about their uncle who is having surgery next week, and would you mind praying for him? Of course, that does not seem unreasonable, but it can add to the feeling that whenever you are in public, you have to be "on" (and if your kids are misbehaving and you are disciplining them with a stern voice, you have to hope that no congregation members are around!).

I believe that most pastors who fall morally are not seeking a relationship. It is that in a moment of emotional vulnerability and exhaustion, when they are depleted, the nurturing attention of someone becomes like water in the desert, and hard to resist. In the midst of caring for everyone else, to have someone express care and concern for you feels a lot like love, and it's powerful. At the very least, it offers a distraction from everyone else's problems.

Dr. Arch Hart, a man whose teaching I greatly respect on this issue, said once at a conference I attended: "A pastor does not fall because he forgets he is a pastor. He falls because he forgets he is human." His point was that though we may be tempted to over-spiritualize the issue, at a basic level we are human beings with emotional needs. It is when we forget that, or neglect it, that we become vulnerable and open to trouble. Of course, I'm sure there is a spiritual component to it as well: The enemy of our souls loves to take down a pastor, and with that, to disappoint and demoralize a whole congregation or denomination.

Bill Hybels of Willow Creek church wrote a brilliant article in Leadership Journal in 1991 in which he talked about checking the gauges on his personal dashboard. In the article he noted that he was diligent about checking the spiritual and the physical gauge, but was unaware that depletion was happening in an area where he wasn't paying attention, namely the emotional gauge.

I learned that I had overlooked an important gauge. The spiritual and physical aspects of life were important, but I had failed to consider another area essential to healthy ministry – emotional strength.

I was so emotionally depleted I couldn't even discern the activity or the call of God on my life. I needed a third gauge on the dashboard of my life.

Throughout a given week of ministry, I slowly began to realize, certain activities drain my emotional reservoir. I now call these experiences IMA's – Intensive Ministry Activities.

An IMA may be a confrontation, an intense counseling session, an exhausting teaching session, or a board meeting about significant financial decisions. Preparing and delivering a message on a sensitive topic, which requires extensive research and thought, for instance, wears me down.

The common denominator of these activities is that they sap you, even in only a few hours.

Every leader constantly takes on IMA's. I didn't realize, however, that I could gauge the degree of their impact on me. As a result, I was oblivious to the intense drain I was experiencing.[7]

The challenge for those of us in the first year of ministry is to identify the activities that are IMAs, those that are emotionally draining for us, and when possible, plan something recuperative or restorative after such activities. It could be something as simple as talking the issue through with your spouse or a trusted friend (of the same sex!), taking a walk and spending time with God, or scheduling your week so that not too many of those IMAs occur in close sequence.

Above all, it is important to acknowledge the existence of the emotional gauge and keep a close watch on it. For some people, who are very in touch with their emotions, that may be an easy gauge for you to read. For others of us, for whom emotion is more under the surface, we may need some help identifying it. Symptoms such as irritability, negativity, or a desire to withdraw or spend time with mindless

---

[7] Hybels, Bill, "Reading Your Gauges," *Leadership Journal*, Spring issue, 1991

activities may be a clue that all is not well emotionally.

If you have a good relationship with other ministers, either in your church or outside it, it would be productive to ask them how they guard against burnout, what signals they pay attention to, and what they have found helpful. That is why having a mentor who is 10-20 years ahead in ministry can be very valuable. A friend of mine makes sure that there is some simple home-improvement job he can complete every week. He does that to offset the feeling that his work is never done, because when you work with people, there is always more to do. Putting in a new doorknob or painting a room can give him a sense of accomplishment, of actually finishing something, that is rare when working with people. Work out what fills your tank emotionally and make sure to include that in your week.

Of course, an emotionally depleted minister is hazardous to his own family, too. If what a wife or children get from their minister husband/father is the dregs, what's left over after a demanding day or week, that is not going to build a healthy family.

A word of caution for the young: It is often the case that pastors in their 20s have an "I'm out of seminary. I'm going to conquer the world by next Monday morning" mentality, and of course, such zeal, energy and enthusiasm are blessings to their church (mostly). However, with the zeal can come a foolish air of invulnerability. To such pastors, I offer these words of biblical wisdom:

"So, if you think you are standing firm, be careful that you don't fall!" (1 Corinthians 10:12).

From my experience in seminary, some of those who were most passionate for Christ, most enthusiastic about entering ministry, those who seemed most diligent in their personal spiritual devotions – they were the ones who ended up falling. I'm not recommending being lukewarm as a protection (God forbid!), but zeal without wisdom is not good enough. From the enemy's perspective, it may be the young hotshots who pose the greatest threat to his kingdom of darkness, and if he can take them out at the very beginning of their ministry, so much the better for him.

Physical Self-Care
One of the occupational hazards of pastors is that we are conditioned to see things through a "spiritual lens" and therefore can sometimes lack common sense. A pastor who is becoming increasingly irritable is not necessarily under specific spiritual attack, but might just be tired. As mentioned above, obesity and overwork are becoming more prevalent in ministry, as well as in other professions. I heard of a retreat center where the first scheduled program event the day after arrival starts at noon, and what most of the pastors do that first morning is simply sleep. They are exhausted, and given a rare chance to recharge and rest, they take it!

God has given us bodies as a resource, and as with all other resources we are given, He expects us to be good stewards. If we neglect a healthy diet, exercise and enough rest, we will of course find ourselves lacking energy, and that physical lack will spill over into other areas of our lives. It is worth asking what we are doing to keep our bodies in good condition, so that we can serve God for as long as he wishes us to.

An exhausted, overweight, "sluggish from fast food" minister is not in an optimal condition to help anybody. It may be that the best cure for our "spiritual" problem may be simply getting enough sleep.

Being disciplined about taking a proper day off every week and taking all the vacation time you are given are also important. We may like to think that it will all collapse without us, but if that is true, then you haven't done a good job delegating or equipping others, and you are in danger of building a ministry around your competency and presence.

The parable of the golden goose seems appropriate here. There was a goose that laid a golden egg every day. Its owners were satisfied with that level of supply for a while, but then they became greedy and decided to cut the goose open to get all the golden eggs at once. Of course, the goose died. To apply that to ministry: You only have so much to give, and if you set the right pace and rhythms to life, you can keep on giving something valuable day after day. However, if you overdo it, if you try to produce all the "golden eggs" of ministry success, you might find yourself dying in the process – either through burnout or through real physical issues and illness.

In the Bible we are given a great example of how exhaustion and a deep emotional toll can lead to despair even when following a great ministry success. In 1 Kings 18, Elijah the prophet has an amazing showdown with the prophets of Baal and Asherah. Elijah wins the 850-to-1 contest easily, and many people turn to the Lord. You would expect him to coast on that ministry success and be emotionally buoyed up for some time, but see what happens just one chapter later:

"He came to a broom tree, sat down under it and prayed that he might die. 'I have had enough, Lord,' he said. 'Take my life; I am no better than my ancestors'" (1 Kings 19:4b).

From basking in triumph to wishing to be dead, in the space of one chapter! What happened? Two things: His life was threatened by Jezebel, and he ran away. The fear (emotional toll) and running away (physical exhaustion) brought him to that point. Ministry success does not inoculate you from the effects of emotional and physical depletion. Take care of yourself!

Spiritual Self-Care

This may seem almost too much of a "given" to include, but we must also take care of ourselves spiritually. Of course, we have a partner in that. God is waiting and willing to sustain us. Elijah's depression and despair were lifted when God allowed him to sleep and then provided food and drink for him by means of an angel. Do you notice that these solutions are not particularly "spiritual" but simply address physical needs?

Others may assume that because we are in ministry, we live in a constant state of blessed awareness of God. Those of us with some experience know that is not true. Although it may be the greatest calling in the world (There's a saying that goes, "When you are called to be a preacher, why stoop to be a king?), the reality is, sometimes it is a grind, it feels just like a job, we are called upon to do things we don't really enjoy, and it can deplete us spiritually.

We are often called upon to advise others on how

to be spiritually healthy, but sometimes we are bad examples, like doctors who smoke. Simply being around "spiritual" stuff does not make us spiritual. Working in a church does not necessarily draw us near to God in the personal, vibrant way He desires.

It is important for each of us to understand our spiritual pathways, the ways God has wired us to enjoy and understand Him. They will vary enormously from person to person. I may feel spiritually stimulated and revived by reading a commentary. You might find standing at the ocean's shore watching a sunset very restoring to your soul. It would not be my place to prescribe exactly what restores your soul, only to encourage you to find out and do it!

Gary Thomas, in his excellent book Sacred Pathways[8], points out eight primary ways in which people connect with God:

- ◆ **Naturalists** – love God in nature, are restored by being outdoors
- ◆ **Sensates** – love the beauty, awe and majesty of God, are drawn to liturgy and beauty
- ◆ **Traditionalists** – love God through rituals and symbols, sacraments and sacrifice
- ◆ **Ascetics** – love God in solitude and simplicity, enjoying times alone in prayer
- ◆ **Activists** – love God through action, challenging injustice and getting their hands dirty
- ◆ **Caregivers** – love God by loving others,

[8] http://www.garythomas.com/sacred-pathways and see Study Guide here: http://assets1.mytrainsite.com/501122/sacredpathways.pdf, with activities for each type

seeing and meeting others' needs
- **Enthusiasts** – love God through mystery and celebration, often through exciting worship
- **Contemplatives** – love God through meditation and deep reflection

The pathways are good to know, for your own personal spiritual vitality and also perhaps to teach your congregation. As I have taught this, it has been a relief for people to discover that there is not a "one size fits all" version of spirituality and that their own preference can be just as valid.

For ministers, constantly dealing with the spiritual, this caution from George MacDonald is a useful warning:

"... for nothing is so deadening to the divine as an habitual dealing with the outsides of holy things ..."[9]

We, as ministers, must work to ensure that the spiritual does not become mundane to us, and the surest way is to work hard at maintaining our own vibrant, spiritual lives. To not do so will surely affect our ministry, and we will find that we are running on empty, preaching on fumes, microwaving old sermons because we have nothing fresh to offer our congregation from our own walk with God.

Mental Self-Care

It is the duty of the pastor to keep his mind sharp. The mind is the primary tool we use to articulate the values and purposes of God. If our thinking becomes

---

[9] MacDonald, George, <u>Thomas Wingfold, Curate</u>, available as an e-book here: http://www.gutenberg.org/ebooks/5976

dull, our presentations will be dull, and we cannot expect a church to get excited about the mediocre vision we present. Some of us are natural readers and learners, and others will need to discipline themselves to seek stimulating inputs.

For myself, having become a Christian at age 20, I always feared becoming irrelevant to those outside the church and having my conversation and sermons restricted to "churchy" topics. I never wanted to alienate myself from the normal, everyday life that most of my congregation experienced. I wanted to be informed about the worlds of politics and business in addition to being theologically competent. These are some of the practices I include in my attempts to keep my mind sharp:

- **Reading** – I keep abreast of the news by reading the BBC World News online (there's an app for that) and reading The Economist magazine weekly. The Economist does have a subscription cost (around $129 per year, but sometimes offered more cheaply), but you can access the website and read many excellent articles for free. I prefer The Economist over strictly American news, since it tends to have a wider, world perspective rather than being so U.S.-centered. Hollywood gossip does not usually make it to the pages of The Economist.

  I try to read about one Christian book per month, usually on the latest trends in ministry (multi-site churches, new methods of discipleship or leadership training, etc.) or on deeper theological issues. As an example, the last few Christian books I have read are:

* Exponential (Dave Ferguson and Jon Ferguson)
* AND: The Gathered and Scattered Church (Hugh Halter and Matt Smay)
* The Big Idea (Dave Ferguson, Jon Ferguson, Eric Bramlett)
* Maximum Faith (George Barna)
* The Power of Vision (George Barna)
* Renovation of the Church (Kent Carlson, Mike Lueken)
* Building a Discipling Culture (Mike Breen)

I also like to read books about human behavior, most recently behavioral economics titles such as Nudge (Richard Thaler, Cass Sunstein) and Predictably Irrational (Dan Ariely). Discovering new perspectives on why people act like they do is always great fodder for sermon material.

* **Television and movies** – I feel compelled to offer a disclaimer at the beginning of this section. Clearly, as ministers, even as Christians, we are called to be "in" the world but not "of" the world, so appropriate boundaries and standards for what we watch are important. I will not try to prescribe for you what yours should be, as we each have our own weaknesses, and that which tempts me may not prove tempting to you. However, be honest with yourself. If your choice of viewing is causing you to sin in your mind, change your viewing habits.

That said, I believe part of our task as preachers is to exegete, or unpack, the culture, and whether we like it or not, television and movies are a massive influence on what is considered normal and acceptable in society. You would only need to look at the changing attitudes toward homosexuality to see what influence the media has recently had, from "Will & Grace" (1998-2006) through to "Modern Family" (2009-) and "Glee" (2009-). If we wish to know which way the wind is blowing in popular opinion, a careful viewing of popular movies and TV shows will be revelatory.

It is all too easy to get involved in the narratives without engaging critical thinking, and I find it helpful to try and create a framework for assessment, from a Christian worldview.

I try to ask three questions of anything I watch:

1. What is the presented problem?
2. What is the proposed solution?
3. To what extent would Christianity agree with these two answers?

♦ **Visiting My Congregation in Their Workplaces** – In order to understand the pressures and situations of my congregation members, I try, when it's possible and practical, to visit them in their places of work, or at the very least, to have good conversations with them about their jobs. Last year, as part of my preparation for a series titled "God @ Work," looking at the character of God through the lens of different professions, I was privileged to spend time in a courtroom with a judge (God as Judge) and in an operating room watching an open-heart operation with a surgeon friend (God as Healer). Both of those experiences were eye-opening, to say the least, and led to great conversations about the challenges of being a Christian in those environments.

Learning to ask good questions is key to that type of research: "Where are you most under pressure in your job? What are the specific challenges to being a Christian in your situation? How do you do this job differently to someone who isn't a Christian?" etc.

♦ **Getting Others' Perspectives** – The reality is that most pastors prepare their messages in isolation, and however skilled they may be, that means your message is from one viewpoint only. More and more pastors are making use of a "teaching team" practice, in which a group of people come together, ideally weeks before a sermon actually has to be preached, and offer input on the topic. In my experience, a mix of clergy and lay people can be most productive, because that saves you from the "ivory tower" syndrome, offering a wider perspective than that of one person who sits in a office reading books. Most pastors in America are white, middle-class males, and there is great benefit in availing yourself of the diversity that is out there – whether that means including people of a different race, gender, life stage, socio-economic status etc.

Proverbs 18:17 states: "The first to present his case seems right, till another comes forward and questions him." In our context, we may feel that our interpretation of a text or our take on a topic is the right one, until we invite the input of others and discover untold riches in a diversity of opinion. Even disagreement over an interpretation can be useful, because it alerts you to a potential conflict in the text to be explored or a tension that needs to be resolved. If someone on your teaching team has questions, it is likely that these same questions will occur to your congregation.

Relational Self-Care

For many individuals, the experience of pastoring is a lonely one. Though we may feel that there is a divine call on our life to ministry, we still have the normal and natural relational needs of every other human being on the planet. For that reason, it's important not to neglect friendships.

In any given week, we will encounter people that drain us, and that tank can only get depleted so far before we feel that we have little to give. It is wise to have friendships that revive you and restore you. For some pastors, it is possible to have deep and honest friendships within the congregation. You will need to be blessed with mature believers who can accept you "out of role," who can understand that church work is not daily bliss, and who can handle it when you are less "pastoral" than others might expect. We all have a desire to be known and accepted for who we truly are, and although we experience that from God, it is truly refreshing when we can find friends in our own church body who can take us that way.

That may not be possible in your situation, though, so you may need to look further afield, perhaps to other pastors in your city who have the ability to understand first-hand the stresses and strains (as well as the joys) of ministry. However you need to do it, establish healthy friendships with people, and preferably those with whom you can talk about the "dark side" of ministry without them throwing up their hands in horror.

I've heard people say that ministry is like a sausage factory. People may enjoy the end product, but they don't really want to know what goes into creating it. There may be staff members who irritate you and congregation members who drain you. To be able to talk about that (without mentioning names) is a helpful pressure relief valve, and the best of friends will not only sympathize with you, but also nudge you gently back in the right direction you if you demonstrate a less-than-godly attitude.

CHAPTER 8:
WEDDINGS

One of the great privileges of being a pastor is that you get to share some of life's most important moments with people, one of which is their wedding day. Sometimes it will be a couple from within the church. Sometimes, someone will have recommended you, and it may be a couple you have never met. In either case, your performance before the wedding, and on the day itself, has the potential to make a big impact on the couple.

The First Meeting

It is my practice to first meet a couple before I agree to marry them. In that way, both you and they have a chance to see whether the right "chemistry" is involved. For example, a couple might want to have a very formal wedding, with little humor, and you might be more of an informal, humorous type of pastor. That would be a mismatch, and it's important to ask the couple early on what the "mood" or style of the ceremony should be. If it doesn't match who you are, then consider referring them to someone who would be a better match for them.

In the initial meeting, I usually provide them with an outline of a typical wedding ceremony, but I emphasize that it is their wedding and I am flexible for whatever they wish to include, such as additional songs, a poem or reading by a friend or family member, etc. Providing such an outline helps them get over the "starting from scratch" fear of not having any idea what to include.

Here is the outline I use for the ceremony:

- Seating of parents
- Pastor, groom and groomsmen enter
- Bridesmaids (and optional flower girl/ring bearer) enter
- Bride enters accompanied by father
- Opening prayer and welcome
- Who gives this woman to be married to this man?
- Groom brings bride forward
- Declaration of intent (the "I do's")
- Pastoral comments (and Bible reading, usually from 1 Corinthians
- 13/Ephesians 5)
- Vows (traditional or written by the couple)
- Exchange of rings
- Optional unity candle or sand ceremony
- Pronouncement ("I now pronounce you ...")
- Kiss
- Presentation ("Mr and Mrs ...")
- Bride and groom exit, followed by wedding party

I also usually encourage them by pointing out that within the ceremony itself, everything they have to do is cued by me, just before they have to do it, so they don't have to hold the whole sequence of events in their memory.

If you charge a fee for your services (pre-marriage counseling, attendance at the rehearsal dinner, the wedding ceremony itself), this is a good time to mention what your fees are. I created a weddings website that contains the fee information, in addition to a sample ceremony order, sample vows and references from couples whom I have married.

Check the logistics around the wedding itself: Will there be a DJ/amplification (i.e., will you need to wear a microphone? If so, try to get a hands-free one, either clip-on or with a stand, so that you don't have to operate one-handed). Are they planning to have a unity candle or sand ceremony as part of the service? Are there relatives who have passed away recently whom they would like mentioned in the opening prayer? ("We would like to remember in prayer Aunt Ethel, who would have loved to be here today, but who we trust is with us in spirit ...").

Pre-Marriage Counseling

I strongly encourage every couple I marry to consider pre-marriage counseling. Most couples lack skills that will be needed to make their marriage excellent, and learning those skills, such as communication and conflict resolution, can make the pathway from singleness to marriage much smoother. I usually point out that when they consider how much they are spending on the wedding and honeymoon (which at the time of writing is usually $15,000-$20,000), then a small investment of time and money in pre-marriage counseling makes a whole lot of sense, and will pay dividends long after the honeymoon is over.

Many excellent pre-marriage counseling resources are available to pastors, but one of the best I have found is called PREPARE/ENRICH (www.prepare-enrich.com). The PREPARE/ENRICH process starts by having the couple take an online assessment, in which they spend 30-45 minutes answering questions about different aspects of their relationship. Based on their answers, a report is created that rates the different areas (communication, conflict resolution, financial management, views on parenting, role relationships, etc.). The report is invaluable for the follow-up counseling sessions, in which the pastor can see at a glance which areas require work and which ones are in a healthy condition. My counseling based on the report usually takes two sessions, at most three. If I feel that the issues require more than three sessions to investigate, I will usually refer them to a professional counselor.

On occasion (maybe 3 percent of the time) the report will reveal such serious difficulties in the relationship that I will refuse to marry the couple at that point and/or require them to get professional counseling. That is a matter of personal conviction that you may not share, but if I see that a planned marriage has a very high chance of failure because of the severity of relational difficulties, then I do not have a clear conscience about performing the ceremony, and thereby declaring the relationship blessed and approved by God.

Naturally, that is both difficult for you to say and hard for a couple to hear, but when you look at the almost equal rate of divorce between Christians and non-Christians, I would suggest that greater caution is required rather than less. When I am explaining my concern to the couple, I would probably put it something like this:

> "The PREPARE/ENRICH report has revealed some serious difficulties in your relationship, which you are both clearly aware of. As your pastor, my concern for you is that you get the best possible start to your married life, and it seems to me that the best chance of that happening would be if you deferred the wedding until after some of these serious issues are worked through with a professional counselor. What are your thoughts on that?"

If there is resistance, and there often is, I follow up with:

> "For me to marry you at this point would be like me driving you to run a marathon when you have a broken foot. You may still want to do it, but I know that there is a very high chance of you experiencing great pain and damage as a result, and I don't want to be an accessory to that. I hope you understand that I am not saying that I will not marry you, but that I have serious reservations about doing that before some of these major issues are worked through."

Sometimes the couple is receptive to that advice; sometimes they are not, and they will proceed to get married without my participation. In other cases, the issues may be minor, and you can address them sufficiently in the two or three sessions you have with the couple, and equip them with some useful tools for their relationship.

In the vast majority of cases, the couple actually find these pre-marriage counseling sessions enjoyable, and they can serve to bring issues to the surface that the couple know they should deal with but haven't had the courage to confront. Having an impartial third party as part of the discussion seems to help.

The Vows

In my initial discussion with the couple, I also ask what vows they wish to use. If they want to use the traditional vows, then I explain that the normal method is for me to read a small part and for them to repeat it after me in the ceremony. They are free just to read it directly from a printed card if they wish, but most couples prefer to simply repeat the vow.

If a couple wishes to use different vows, or write their own, then the procedure is slightly different. I ask them to let me know ahead of time, by e-mailing a copy of the vows to me. I also tell them to print out their vows on a card and bring them with them to the rehearsal and the ceremony. I print a copy for myself and bring it with me on the wedding day just so that, horror of horrors, if they forgot their card, I can smoothly bring it out of my pocket and hand it to them, and the service continues without an embarrassing delay.

The Rehearsal and Rehearsal Dinner

Some pastors choose not to attend a rehearsal, confident that having discussed the order of service in detail with the couple, nothing additional really needs to be done. For myself, I see my attendance at the rehearsal as helpful in calming the nerves of the couple and a chance to run through the service with me present, which is more realistic. I generally choose not to attend the dinner part of the evening, unless I am already close with the couple and considered a friend. They may invite you as a matter of courtesy, but it is usually not viewed as impolite just to attend the rehearsal part of the evening. I ask the couple to bring the wedding license to the rehearsal dinner and to hand it off to me there. That gives them one less thing to think about on the big day.

In most cases, the couple will have a wedding coordinator whose job it is to tell people (primarily the wedding party) when to enter, where to stand, when to exit. If the couple does not have a wedding coordinator, that role may fall to you, and you may need to advise. Here are a few pro tips that will let the party know that you know what you are doing:

- Tell the groomsmen to all position their hands the same way, whether that is right over left in front, or behind – whatever it is, they should all match.
- Tell everyone that their eyes should basically follow the bride – wherever she is, that's where they should be looking.
- Tell the bridesmaids and groomsmen not to lock their knees, which can cause fainting. They should flex their legs every now and then when standing in place.
- When father and bride are in place, the father should lift the bride's veil (if she has one), kiss

her cheek, and then turn to shake the hand of the approaching groom.

* Remind the maid of honor to take the bride's bouquet when she walks forward to stand in front of the minister – that thing can get heavy.

* Tell the bride and groom not to force the ring onto their partner's finger if it gets stuck at the knuckle, but to simply push it to where it can comfortably go, and then let them fix it discreetly when no one is looking

What To Share in the Ceremony

The pastor in a wedding has the opportunity to share a few words of encouragement with the couple about the true meaning of love and marriage. Unless the couple specifically requests it, I do not generally use the opportunity to give an explicit gospel message. There will be a few subtle points made within the wedding message about Christ describing the church as His bride and explaining that His love extended so far as to even die for her, and so on – but there is nothing that would usually make people of other faiths, or no faith, uncomfortable. I build my message around one of two Bible passages: the great chapter on love in 1 Corinthians 13, and the other on the duty of husbands and wives in Ephesians 5.

In order to make the wedding distinctive, prior to the ceremony I ask the couple to share with me a story that will give some insight into their relationship. It could be how they first met, their first impressions of each other, a funny date, the proposal, etc. At the beginning of my wedding message, I retell that story, which serves a couple of useful functions.

First, it relaxes the couple and reduces the stress they feel standing there for the big moment. Second, for those in the congregation who know them less well, it offers a window of insight and understanding into who they are as a couple. Third, it makes the wedding message unique. Even though I will use components of other wedding messages I have spoken, this part will be completely unique to them, and it will make it more memorable. I have had many people compliment me on how personal and fitting the wedding message was, and many referrals come precisely because of that "tailor-made" approach to what is shared.

The Wedding Day

My checklist for the day of the wedding goes something like this:

- Double-check the time and location of the wedding (usually same place as rehearsal).
- Make sure all wedding clothing (shoes, tie, etc.) are available and clean.
- Put some tissues in your pocket, to be offered in case of excessive weeping by bride or groom.
- Check that you have the wedding message and order of service in Bible/wedding book.
- Make sure you have the wedding license and mailing envelope.
- Print out the map/directions to wedding. (Plan to arrive 45 minutes to one hour before the start of the ceremony. That gives you enough "buffer" time for emergencies such as your car breaking down. Also, the couple can

become nervous if they don't see you until just before the start of the ceremony.)

♦ When you arrive at the wedding site, find the groom (usually easier to locate than the bride, who is hidden away somewhere) and let him know you have arrived.

♦ If you are going to need a microphone, find the DJ/sound person and get set up.

♦ Check your environment – where you will stand, lectern, etc.

♦ Make sure the best man (or whoever is supposed to) has the rings.

Sequence of Meetings

This is the approximate sequence and timing of meetings/contacts you should plan to have with the couple:

♦ Initial meeting

♦ Pre-marriage counseling session 1 (2 weeks after initial meeting)

♦ Pre-marriage counseling session 2 (1-2 weeks after Session 1)

♦ Meeting/contact to get "personal story" for wedding message (2 weeks before wedding)

CHAPTER 9:
FUNERALS

At a Time Like This ...

There is hardly any other experience for which your helpful presence will be remembered and appreciated more than following the death of a loved one. It is normal to feel some anxiety about entering such a potentially emotionally-charged situation. We wonder if we will know what to say, if our words will bring comfort or if they will just ring hollow. In situations in which the death is particularly tragic, for example in the case of a young child, it is not uncommon to feel that there is nothing useful that you can offer.

However, do not underestimate the power of a non-anxious presence. If you can at least be somewhat calm in the midst of extreme emotion, you can provide a temporary oasis of stability. Also remember that despite your strong instincts to do so, it is not your responsibility to make anyone feel better. It is that urge that leads less-experienced pastors to utter trite and offensive clichés such as,

"He is in a better place," or "God must have wanted her more in heaven than on earth." Really, if platitudes such as those spring to mind, then you are probably better not speaking at all.

Grief is painful and urgent, and not cured or alleviated with a few clever phrases. Allow people to grieve. Do not make them think that their raw emotion is unpleasant or threatening to you (even though it may be.) If you are particularly empathetic, you might find yourself weeping with the family, and that is not a problem unless your weeping is so great that they seek to comfort you!

The Funeral Service

The key to a "good" funeral, as it is with weddings, is personalization. As far as possible, avoid the generic. Yes, there may be a rough outline of a typical funeral service that you and the family will wish to follow, but a service is made more meaningful the more personal it is. If there is music or literature that was loved by the deceased, it can be played or read. If there are pictures, they can be displayed or made into a slideshow to be shown prior to, and/or after, the service. If there are family members or friends who wish to say a few words of tribute or appreciation, then that can be included. Your task as the minister is to enable the family to say a meaningful goodbye.

What To Share in the Funeral Message

What to share is largely dictated by whether the person was known to be a Christian or not. If the person was a believer, then you'll have an opportunity to speak with confidence about that person's faith and about Jesus' promises of the eternal destination that awaits those who trust in Him.

If the person was not a believer, or his or her spiritual state is unknown to you, then you will have to be more vague and circumspect. In such a situation, it is perhaps better to focus on what the person was known for, and on the individual's good character (if that was indeed the case.)

A word of advice: When you mention the person in your message, be sure to use the name by which he or she was commonly known. You can ascertain that by asking the family. He may have been officially named "John," but if everyone called him "Jack," and you keep referring to him as "John," that will just emphasize the fact that you didn't really know him, and it will alienate you from family and friends who did.

Follow-Up

It is tempting to think that once the funeral service and reception are over, your work as pastor is done. I recommend that a couple of months following the funeral, you pay a visit to the bereaved and ask how they are doing. Usually, in the first few weeks following a person's death, family members are surrounded by other family members and friends. Gradually, however, the concern wears off, and people go about their everyday lives. It is in that period that grief can hit hardest, when the support systems are gone. In that time, it can be critical for a pastor to express continued concern.

If your church has a group for individuals in the pain of grief (such as GriefShare), then make the person aware of that ministry. There are also some useful books that you can recommend, such as Grieving the Loss of Someone You Love: Daily

<u>Meditations to Help You Through the Grieving Process</u> by Ray Mitsch[10]. In addition, if you have an electronic calendar, set a reminder for a few days prior to the anniversary of the person's death. When that time comes, simply saying something like, "I know this might be a hard week for you. I'll be praying for you" can mean a lot.

---

[10] Mitsch, Ray, Grieving the Loss of Someone You Love: Daily Meditations to Help You Through the Grieving Process, Vine Books, Ann Arbor, MI, 1993

CHAPTER 10:
HOSPITAL VISITS

Depending on the age and wellness of your congregation, hospital visits could be a major or minor part of your ministry. In either case, it is yet another opportunity to be with people at a critical, and often worrying, part of their life. You have the chance to bring peace into an otherwise anxious situation.

My practice when I arrive at the hospital is simply to offer a prayer as I walk from the parking lot, asking God to use me to bring some comfort and encouragement to both the person who is sick, and the family/friends who may be there.

I ascertain from hospital reception the location of the patient and then get to that floor. Somewhere between reception and the room I find either a bathroom where I can wash my hands or a hand sanitization station to make sure that I am not bringing unnecessary germs into what should be a sanitary environment. When arriving on the floor, I check with the nurses' station to make sure that it is OK to visit right then, and tell the nurses that I am the patient's pastor. You want to make sure that you are not intruding while the person is in the middle of some procedure.

If I am given permission to visit, I knock on the door, announce myself and ask if it is OK to come in. If it is, then I approach the bed and introduce myself to any others that are around the person. Assuming that they are non-contagious, and if appropriate, I shake the person's hand or make some physical contact. I then make some generic inquiry about the patient's condition, such as "What's going on with you?" or "How are you feeling?" and let the person share whatever specifics he or she is willing to share.

After that, it's pretty much a "play it by ear" situation. I try to remain not longer than 15 minutes, since most people in the hospital feel tired when they are sick, unless the person makes it clear that he welcomes the company and will be bored if you go. Inquire if there is anything you can bring, such as a magazine, a Bible, some candy. If nothing else, then ask if you can pray, and offer a brief prayer asking wisdom for the doctors and healing from the Lord, whether by means of medicine or miracle. Promise to check back in a couple of days. Then call daily if you can and visit every three or four days if possible.

Again, this is one of those situations that people remember. You may feel that all you did was pop in briefly, offer a few words and pray, but the visit by the pastor at a time of life marked by fear and vulnerability will not be forgotten.

CHAPTER 11:
CONFLICT

It's Going To Happen

Since we live in a fallen, sinful world, and since that fallen sinfulness extends also to Christians, it is only to be expected that conflict will happen. We each come with our own particular mix of brokenness, quirks, imperfections, preferences, and at some point they are bound to clash. In your ministry career you can expect to clash with members of the congregation as well as your own staff members.

I hope you are not entering ministry with the naïve idea that working on a church staff is some kind of heaven on earth. If that is what you expect, you are in for a rude awakening. Yes, it is hoped that you will be part of a team of people passionately engaged in extending the Kingdom of God. However, there definitely will be times when you "push each other's buttons" and engage in unhealthy conflict. On the positive side, those are opportunities to practice the ministry of reconciliation with which we are all tasked. On the negative side, such situations can be a great cause of bitterness and the primary reason why people leave church staff.

The Biblical Model

Our starting point for dealing with conflict must be the Scriptures. Because the Bible is a very practical book, it provides a process for resolving conflict, found in Matthew 18:15-17.

"If your brother sins against you, go and show him his fault, just between the two of you. If he listens to you, you have won your brother over. But if he will not listen, take one or two others along, so that 'every matter may be established by the testimony of two or three witnesses.' If he refuses to listen to them, tell it to the church; and if he refuses to listen even to the church, treat him as you would a pagan or a tax collector."

Some initial points are clear: If you feel sinned against, do not gossip about it or attempt to damage anyone else's reputation. In general, the issue should not be discussed with anyone else, with perhaps one exception. If you are uncertain about whether your negative reaction to that person's actions or words is reasonable, you might wish to confide in a trusted accountability partner or friend, and get a second opinion. That should not be used as an excuse to get another person on your side, or persuade that person to share your view of this terrible person who has offended you. It is a genuine attempt to achieve objectivity, with a willingness to have your view of events corrected if your trusted person interprets the situation differently or thinks you are overreacting.

In addition, if you remain persuaded that you have

been sinned against, you go directly to the other person with the specific and genuine end goal of reconciliation. The point is to keep the situation at the lowest level, without escalating or increasing the number of people involved. I would suggest at the initial meeting that you go in with some delicacy, and ask questions such as, "It seems that we are at odds with each other right now, and I don't want that to continue. I want us to be in good relationship with each other, so if there's something I've done that has offended you, or if there's something between us, can we talk it out?" With that opening, you have made it clear that your priority is to restore the relationship, not to score points or force a confession from the other person. If nothing specific is elicited, then you might need to be more specific yourself in telling the person why there is an issue.

Allow for the fact that someone may have misinterpreted something, or misunderstood, and clarification might solve the whole problem. As a general rule, use "I" and "I feel" statements, which are less accusatory than "You" statements. "When you seemed to ignore me at the potluck, I felt that perhaps there was something between us. Am I right with that, or is it nothing?" "When you ignored me at the potluck, my feelings were hurt. Is there something I have done that ..." Those less-confrontational openings create better soil for reconciliation than an accusation would.

If you are unsuccessful at that level, and reconciliation or agreement cannot be achieved, then you are allowed to take it to the next level. When choosing who to accompany you, try to select people who would be viewed as neutral by the other party. If you bring your best friends, or your greatest supporters in the church, the other person will feel ganged up on, and an attitude of defensiveness is more likely.

The thoughts above all relate to issues of a more personal nature. In ministry, the conflict will often come over ministry-related decisions, with members of the congregation, and that is what we will deal with next.

Conflict With Members of the Congregation (MOTC)

In my experience the primary cause of conflict with MOTC is lack of clear communication and/or misunderstanding. Nine out of 10 times that sort of conflict can be positively resolved with an appropriate listening, non-combative attitude – although it may take some doing. Our natural response when someone is upset with us is to become defensive or to counter-attack. That serves only to escalate the situation, and makes it worse than it might have been.

Proper preparation and prayer are needed in order to avoid such natural responses. You need to pray and work yourself into a listening attitude, being willing to fully hear what the other person is saying before responding. And this is key: You respond rather than react. The calmness of spirit necessary for such encounters is really only achieved through prayer and a strong sense of God's approval of you. Only with that sense of security can you respond from a place of calm.

When the appointment begins, if you feel it is appropriate, ask permission to open with a prayer. In that prayer, express a desire for clear understanding and a right heart, and acknowledge the relationship that exists between you. A sample prayer might be as follows:

"God, we thank you that you have promised to be with us today. We pray for your Holy Spirit to guide us and direct us. We ask that if there is anything between us, at the end of our time together, You bring us together as brother to brother (or sister) in Christ. Please lead us now. In Jesus' name. Amen."

As the conversation starts, what you are trying to do is understand the motive of the other person. Why is he or she upset? What exactly is bothering the person? Often it might be that a cherished program or ministry is being changed or removed. The positive attitude to take toward that is to acknowledge that the person actually cares about the church, about what happens in the church. That is, in itself, a good thing, and far better than apathy or disinterest. It is generally people who feel invested who complain when they perceive that something they value is being threatened.

My initial response, after hearing the individual's case/complaint is to say something like, "It's clear that you care deeply about this church/ministry. That's something I'm thankful for. I'm grateful that you are so invested that you want to talk to me about this. Thank you for coming to me directly rather than simply being unhappy and expressing that around the church. That takes courage and obedience, and I want you to know I appreciate that."

With that opening, whether you agree with the complaint or not, you have made two positive comments:

- The person is invested in the church or ministry.

♦ The person has not gossiped but has come to you directly.

The fact that you have responded the way you have is probably different than what the person expected. He or she may have come looking for, or expecting, a fight, and you have opened up with two compliments. That should serve to initially defuse the situation.

Ask good questions, making sure that you really understand the individual's concern. A frequent complaint from those who leave churches is that they did not feel listened to. You may actually have 27 good reasons why you want to cancel that ministry, but the other person may not be in a frame of mind to hear any of them. Remember, this is not a case of "the one with the best arguments wins." As Christians, and particularly as pastors, what we wish to communicate is love and care. We might easily win an argument but lose the person in the process. Honestly, sometimes it might be right to lose a person, but let's not do it because we were sinful and defensive. Let it at least be an honest and respectful disagreement over direction, rather than in response to a personal affront.

Try to find areas of agreement. You may, for instance, be able to agree on the goal of the church or general area of ministry, even while disagreeing on method.

Watch your tone. If the person is interested in why you reached the decision you did, then you can explain. The tone you use is critically important. If you are condescending, defensive or even aggressive, seeming like you are trying to win a debate, there is little chance of it going well. Try to be more tentative, using phrases such as, "I hoped that if we ...," or "My goal in doing this was _____, but it sounds like you have some hesitation about that. Now, if I'm about to make a mistake, or there is something I haven't thought of, I really do need to know, and if you can help me with that ..."

The point is to try to mentally see yourself on the same side of the table as this MOTC, facing the issue/problem that is opposite you both. The sense you are trying to create is that you are on a team together, trying to work out the best way forward. If, in the conversation, the person does point out something you hadn't thought of, then acknowledge that and thank the person. In doing so, you are creating an ally rather than an opponent.

Do not try to resolve conflict through e-mail. Although we may think that we can more clearly express ourselves in written communication, e-mail lacks the emotional cues of tone and facial expression. Something that could have been softened with a smile or a gentle tone, is presented in its raw, direct form in an e-mail – and it is in vain to say that you didn't mean it to be taken that way. (Also, you don't want the paper trail, in case you word something foolishly or awkwardly. In person, you can correct a mis-statement you've just made. That is not possible with an e-mail.) The only acceptable use of e-mail in a conflict situation is for logistics, to arrange a time to meet the person face to face.

A word of caution: Sometimes the stated issue is not the real issue, and it will take some probing and discernment to discover "the issue behind the issue." In such a situation, a genuine expression of pastoral concern can go a long way. Even when I know a person is coming to see me about a specific issue, I will still open up with something more generic like, "So, how has life been treating you lately?" just to get an idea of the frame of mind that recent circumstances have created. Sometimes, when I have called the meeting, and feel I need to confront the MOTC about something, even asking this generic question had led to a person openly admitting a fault, confessing and asking for forgiveness – far better than if I had started with, "Let me tell you why I am not pleased with you and your actions!"

If you are new to a church and don't know the person very well, it might be wise prior to the appointment to ask another staff member what they he or she knows about the individual. There might have some insight that is useful to know, such as, "He has run off the last three pastors," or "She has been really unhappy about the change in worship style." That can help you know what you might be encountering, and what a good approach might be. You might also be surprised, and the issue may be something completely different.

Conflict With Another Staff Member

This is painful when it happens, but it will happen. In general, the conflict resolution process of Matthew 18, and advice given above connected to that, is just as relevant. It is critical to realize that conflict with another staff member cannot simply be ignored or swept under the rug. We cannot expect God to bless our ministry if we are ignoring such an important issue. As the letter of 1 John says, Anyone who claims to be in the light but hates his brother is still in the darkness (1 John 2:9).

Many of us in the pastoral profession do not like conflict. We seek to avoid it, but allowing conflict to fester and remain unresolved creates a playground for the devil. It has to be addressed, in a direct and godly manner. You may think that the conflict does not need to affect your ministry, but it inevitably will. Since conflict within a staff team is so serious, it may require the intervention of a senior staff member if resolution between you and the other person is not achieved between the two of you. If you are, in fact, the senior staff member or senior pastor, then you may need to ask for asking the assistance of your elders or board.

Resources
Conflict in itself is neutral. How it is handled makes the difference. There are two resources that I think will be particularly helpful to you, as you seek to create a harmonious staff team that deals with conflict in a productive and healthy way. My primary resource is the book, and accompanying workbook, **The Five Dysfunctions of a Team** by Patrick Lencioni (Jossey Bass, 2002). Having applied the book's principles in real-life staff conflict situations, I can attest to their usefulness. In fact, this book and the principles it contains are so helpful that I would consider it required reading for anyone who has any type of responsibility for a team.

The second resource is **The Unity Factor: Developing a Healthy Leadership Team** by Larry Osborne (Owl's Nest, 2006) and the third, also by Osborne is **Sticky Teams** (Zondervan, 2010) Larry Osborne's experience is directly that of a pastor, and his book contains extremely valuable advice for anyone trying to build a healthy leadership team within the church.

In summary, I think it is important to remember that we are on the same team. If you have conflict with any other Christian, whether it is a member of the congregation or another staff member, it is always civil war. Any pastor who wishes to succeed must develop the skill of mastering conflict, as it will always be there and can make or break a ministry. I will leave the last words of this chapter to David – king, psalmist, and a man who was ever so familiar with conflict:

> *Psalm 133*
>
> *1 How good and pleasant it is*
> > *when brothers live together in unity!*
> *2 It is like precious oil poured on the head,*
> > *running down on the beard,*
> > *running down on Aaron's beard,*
> > *down upon the collar of his robes.*
> *3 It is as if the dew of Hermon*
> > *were falling on Mount Zion.*
> > *For there the Lord bestows his blessing,*
> > *even life forevermore.*

CONCLUSION

The work of a pastor is both challenging and immensely rewarding. We will not know fully, this side of heaven, what impact we have had in people's lives. It is my hope that something in this volume has proved helpful for you and will better equip you, as you depend on the Holy Spirit, to be a faithful and effective minister for Jesus Christ.

My last piece of advice for you is to adopt the mindset of a continual learner. God, circumstances and other people will continue to teach you as long as you are humble enough, and eager enough, to learn and grow into the pastor God desires you to be.

May God strengthen you with all power and equip you with all wisdom as you live out this privileged calling.

GLYN NORMAN

ABOUT THE AUTHOR

Glyn Norman has worked in the business world, for the British Government, as a church planter in Berlin, Germany and as a pastor in California and Florida. In preparation for ministry, he attended London Bible College (now London School of Theology) where he achieved an honors degree in Theology.

With over 20 years' ministry experience, Glyn realized that there was much to being an effective pastor that was not taught in seminary, and out of that realization, this book was born.

Glyn is the husband of but one wife, Cathleen, and the father of Landon and Cicely. His interests include exegeting popular culture, listening to 80s and baroque classical music, reading The Economist, Star Trek (The Next Generation), soccer (English, of course) and table tennis (which he claims is a real sport).

GLYN NORMAN

RESOURCES LIST

For quick access to the resources recommended in this book, go to http://firstyearinministry.com and click the Resources link.

A small commission for resources purchased through that site goes to the author. Thank you.

TESTIMONIALS

Although seminaries drill the budding minister in theology, homiletics and parsing verbs, they generally fall dreadfully short in equipping a neophyte pastor to navigate through the muddled maze of ministry, the minefield of church politics and the daily grind of the mundane. This book is a gold mine of practical, hands-on, and gut-level advice and help for ministers of the gospel. Reading this book before I entered the ministry would have saved me a lot of time, stress and headaches.

Richard Chip Kirk
International Minister, Operation Mobilization

I have known Glyn for over 20 years. Even as a 'boy' in seminary he was able to speak into situations with refreshing simplicity and clarity. Nothing has changed, except perhaps for a lot more grey hairs caused by the years of ministry experience needed to write this book. If you want to stave off the grey hairs and thrive in ministry, this easy to read book will be worth the investment.

Craig Rees
Lead Pastor, South Tampa Fellowship, Tampa, FL

CPSIA information can be obtained
at www.ICGtesting.com
Printed in the USA
LVOW13s1715171217
560080LV00001B/71/P